Experiences in Groups

AND OTHER PAPERS

W. R. BION

London and New York

First published in 1961 by
Tavistock Publications Limited

Reprinted seven times

Reprinted 1989, 1991, 1992, 1994 by Routledge
11 New Fetter Lane
London EC4P 4EE

Simultaneously published in the USA and Canada
by Routledge
29 West 35th Street, New York, NY 10001

© Tavistock Publications Limited 1961

Printed in Great Britain by
J. W. Arrowsmith Ltd, Bristol

A Tavistock/Routledge publication

ISBN 0-415-04020-5

Experiences in Groups

Y

12

Contents

Acknowledgements

Thanks are due to the following for permission to reprint the papers collected in this volume: the Editor of the *Lancet* in respect of 'Intra-Group Tensions in Therapy' (*Lancet*, 27 November 1943); the publisher and the Editorial Committee of *Human Relations* in respect of 'Experiences in Groups, I—VII' (*Human Relations*, Vols. I—IV, 1948-1951); the Editor of the *International Journal of Psycho-Analysis* in respect of 'Group Dynamics: a Re-view' (*International Journal of Psycho-Analysis*, Vol. XXXIII, Pt. 2, 1952).

Introduction

The articles printed here aroused more interest than I expected; consequently there have been requests for reprints which it has been impossible to supply from the stock available.

The solution, as I now realize, would have been to re-publish them at the outset. I was reluctant to do this without changes embodying later experience. However, rewriting is seldom successful, and much can be lost by the exclusion of tentative theories that show how ideas were developed. The articles are therefore reprinted without alteration. It will be seen that two do not belong to the series that originally appeared in *Human Relations*; the first is reprinted because it throws light on the origins of my belief that this approach merited further trial, and the last because it summarizes conclusions that I would like to have taken further, and that others might like to develop. I have also a purely personal reason for wishing to acknowledge the collaboration with John Rickman and the inspiration which his generosity and enthusiasm always engendered.

I regret not having discussed sovereignty and power. In small groups like those used here, power and sovereignty do not develop to maturity. The mature form is extrinsic and impinges on the group only in the form of invasion by another group. These matters I shall discuss in a further volume, if I have time, and I shall then take up the extra-economic sources of the value of money, which not only are important in themselves but also contribute significantly through their influence on economics to the dynamics of sovereignty and power.

I am impressed, as a practising psycho-analyst, by the fact that the psycho-analytic approach, through the individual, and the approach these papers describe, through the group, are dealing with different facets of the same phenomena. The two methods provide the practitioner with a rudimentary binocular vision. The observations tend to fall into two categories, whose affinity is shown by phenomena which, when examined by one method, centre on the Œdipal situation, related to the pairing group, and, when examined by the other, centre on the sphinx, related to problems of knowledge and scientific method.

My present work, which I hope to publish, convinces me of the central importance of the Kleinian theories of projective identification and the interplay between the paranoid-schizoid and depressive positions.

Without the aid of these two sets of theories I doubt the possibility of any advance in the study of group phenomena. The part played by the mechanisms to which these theories relate is adumbrated in the last chapter, to which I commend your attention.

W. R. BION

Pre-View

153

Intra-Group Tensions in Therapy

Their study as the task of the group[1]

The term 'group therapy' can have two meanings. It can refer to the treatment of a number of individuals assembled for special therapeutic sessions, or it can refer to a planned endeavour to develop in a group the forces that lead to smoothly running co-operative activity.

The therapy of individuals assembled in groups is usually in the nature of explanation of neurotic trouble, with reassurance; and sometimes it turns mainly on the catharsis of public confession. The therapy of groups is likely to turn on the acquisition of knowledge and experience of the factors which make for a good group spirit.

A SCHEME FOR REHABILITATION (W. R. B.)

In the treatment of the individual, neurosis is displayed as a problem of the individual. In the treatment of a group it must be displayed as a problem of the group. This was the aim I set myself when I was put in charge of the training wing of a military psychiatric hospital. My first task, there-

---

[1] Written in collaboration with John Rickman, M.D.

fore, was to find out what the pursuit of this aim would mean in terms of time-table and organization.

I was not able to work at this task in an atmosphere of cloistered calm. No sooner was I seated before desk and papers than I was beset with urgent problems posed by importunate patients and others. Would I see the NCOs in charge of the training wing and explain to them what their duties were? Would I see Private A who had an urgent need for 48 hours' leave to see an old friend just back from the Middle East? Private B, on the other hand, would seek advice because an unfortunate delay on the railway had laid him open to misunderstanding as one who had overstayed his leave. And so on.

An hour or so of this kind of thing convinced me that what was required was discipline. Exasperated at what I felt to be a postponement of my work, I turned to consider this problem.

DISCIPLINE FOR THE NEUROTIC

Under one roof were gathered 300-400 men who in their units already had the benefit of such therapeutic value as lies in military discipline, good food, and regular care; clearly this had not been enough to stop them from finding their way into a psychiatric hospital. In a psychiatric hospital such types provide the total population and by the time they reach the training wing they are not even subject to such slight restraint as is provided by being confined to bed.

I became convinced that what was required was the sort of discipline achieved in a theatre of war by an experienced officer in command of a rather scallywag battalion. But what sort of discipline is that? In face of the urgent need for action I sought, and found, a working hypothesis. It was, that the discipline required depends on two main factors: (i) the presence of the enemy, who provided a common danger and a common aim; and (ii) the presence of an officer who, being experienced, knows some of his own failings, respects the integrity of his men, and is not afraid of either their good-will or their hostility.

An officer who aspires to be the psychiatrist in charge of a rehabilitation wing must know what it is to be in a responsible position at a time when responsibility means having to face issues of life and death. He must know what it is to exercise authority in circumstances that make his fellows unable to accept his authority except in so far as he appears to be able to sustain it. He must know what it is to live in close emotional relationship with his fellow men. In short, he must know the sort of life that is led by a combatant officer. A psychiatrist who knows this will at least be spared the hideous blunder of thinking that patients are potential cannon-fodder, to be returned as such to their units. He will realize that it is his task to produce self-respecting men socially adjusted to the community and therefore willing to accept its responsibilities whether in peace or war. Only thus will he be free from deep feelings of guilt that effectually stultify any efforts he may otherwise make towards treatment.

What common danger is shared by the men in the rehabilitation wing? What aim could unite them?

There was no difficulty about detecting a common danger; neurotic extravagances of one sort and another perpetually endanger the work of the psychiatrist or of any institution set up to further treatment of neurotic disorders. The common danger in the training wing was the existence of neurosis as a disability of the community. I was now back at my starting-point—the need, in the treatment of a group, for displaying neurosis as a problem of the group. But, thanks to my excursion into the problem of discipline, I had come back with two additions. Neurosis needs to be displayed as a danger to the group; and its display must somehow be made the common aim of the group.

But how was the group to be persuaded to tackle neurotic disability as a communal problem?

The neurotic patient does not always want treatment, and when at last his distress drives him to it he does not want it wholeheartedly. This reluctance has been recognized in the discussion of resistance and allied phenomena; but the existence of comparable phenomena in societies has not been recognized.

Society has not yet been driven to seek treatment of its psychological disorders by psychological means because it has not achieved sufficient insight to appreciate the nature of its distress. The organization of the training wing had to be such that the growth of insight should at least not be hindered. Better still if it could be designed to throw into prominence the way in which neurotic behaviour adds to the difficulties of the community, destroying happiness and efficiency. If communal distress were to become demonstrable as a neurotic by-product, then neurosis itself would be seen to be worthy of communal study and attack. And a step would have been taken on the way to overcoming resistance in the society.

Two minor, but severely practical, military requirements had to be satisfied by the training wing. The organization should if possible provide a means by which the progress of the patients could be indicated, so that the psychiatrist could tell if a man were fit for discharge. It would also be useful to have an indication of the patient's direction, of his effective motivation, so that an opinion could be formed about the sort of work to which he should be discharged.

I found it helpful to visualize the projected organization of the training wing as if it were a framework enclosed within transparent walls. Into this space the patient would be admitted at one point, and the activities within that space would be so organized that he could move freely in any direction according to the resultant of his conflicting impulses. His movements, as far as possible, were not to be distorted by outside interference. As a result, his behaviour could be trusted to give a fair indication of his effective will and aims, as opposed to the aims he himself proclaimed or the psychiatrist wished him to have.

It was expected that some of the activities organized within the 'space' would be clearly warlike, others equally clearly civilian, others again merely expressions of neurotic powerlessness. As the patient's progress was seen to run along one or other of these paths, so his 'assets and liabilities', to use a phrase employed in the sphere of officer selection by Major Eric Wittkower, could be assessed with reasonable objectivity. As his progress appeared to be towards one or other.of the possible exits from this imaginary space, so his true aim could be judged.

At the same time the organization could be used to further the main aim of the training wing—the education and training of the community in the problems of interpersonal relationships. If it could approximate to this theoretical construct it would enable the members of the training wing to stand (as it were) outside the framework and look with detachment and growing understanding upon the problems of its working.

THE EXPERIMENT

The training wing, consisting of some hundred men, was paraded and was told that in future the following regulations would apply:

1. Every man must do one hour's physical training daily unless a medical certificate excused him.

2. Every man must be a member of one or more groups—the groups designed to study handicrafts, Army correspondence courses, carpentry, map-reading, sand-tabling, etc.

3. Any man could form a fresh group if he wanted to do so, either because no group existed for his particular activity or because, for some reason or other, he was not able to join an existing similar group.

4. A man feeling unable to attend his group would have to go to the rest-room.

5. The rest-room would be in charge of a nursing orderly, and must be kept quiet for reading, writing, or games such as draughts. Talking in an undertone was permitted with the permission of the nursing orderly but other patients must not be disturbed; couches were provided so that any men who felt unfit for any activity whatever could lie down. The nursing orderly would take the names of all those in the rest-room as a matter of routine.

It was also announced that a parade would be held every day at 12.10 p.m. for making announcements and conducting other business of the training wing. Unknown to the patients, it was intended that this meeting, strictly limited to 30 minutes, should provide an occasion for the men to step outside their framework and look upon its working with the detachment of spectators. In short, it was intended to be the first step towards the elaboration of therapeutic seminars.

For the first few days little happened; but it was evident that among the patients a great deal of discussion and thinking was taking place. The first few 12.10 meetings were little more than attempts to guage the sincerity of the proposals; then the groups began to form in earnest. Among the more obvious activities there was a programme group to chart out working hours of groups and their location, to make announcements, and to allocate tickets for free concerts and such-like. In a very short time the programme room, which showed by means of flags on a work-chart the activities of every man in the training wing, now growing rapidly in size, became almost vernal in its display of multi-coloured flags of patterns suggested by the ingenuity of the patients. By a happy thought a supply of flags bearing the skull and crossbones was prepared, ready for the use of such gentlemen as felt compelled to be absent without leave.

The existence of this brave display gave occasion for what was probably the first important attempt at therapeutic co-operation at a 12.10 meeting. It had been my habit, on going the rounds of the groups, to detach one or two men from their immediate work and take them with me 'just to see how the rest of the world lives'. I was therefore able to communicate to this meeting an interesting fact observed by myself and by others who had gone round with me. Namely, that, although there were many groups and almost entire freedom to each man to follow the bent of his own inclinations, provided he could make a practical proposal, yet very little was happening. The carpenter's shop might have one or two men at most; car maintenance the same; in short, I suggested, it almost looked as if the training wing was a façade with nothing behind it. This, I said, seemed odd because I remembered how bitterly the patients in the training wing had previously complained to me that one of their objections to the Army was the 'eyewash'. Its presence in the training wing, therefore, really did seem to be a point worth study and discussion.

This announcement left the audience looking as if they felt they were being 'got at'. I turned the discussion over at that point as a matter of communal responsibility and not

2

something that concerned myself, as an officer, alone.

With surprising rapidity the training wing became self-critical. The freedom of movement permitted by the original set-up allowed the characteristics of a neurotic community to show with painful clarity; within a few days men complained that the wards (hitherto always claimed to be spotless) were dirty and could not be kept clean under the present system of a routine hour for ward fatigues. They asked and were allowed to organize under the programme group an 'orderly group', whose duties it would be to keep the wards clean throughout the day. The result of this was that on a subsequent weekly inspection the Commanding Officer of the hospital remarked on the big change in cleanliness that had taken place.

SOME RESULTS

It is impossible to go into details about the working of all the therapeutic aspects of the organization; but two examples of method and result may be given.

Shortly after the new arrangement started, men began to complain to me that patients were taking advantage of the laxity of the organization. 'Only 20 per cent,' they said, 'of the men are taking part and really working hard; the other 80 per cent are just a lot of shirkers.' They complained that not only was the rest-room often filled with people simply loafing, but that some men even cut that. I was already aware of this, but refused, at least outwardly, to have its cure made my responsibility. Instead, I pointed out that, at an Army Bureau of Current Affairs meeting some weeks before, the discussion had at one point centred on just that question— namely, the existence in communities (and the community then under discussion was Soviet Russia) of just such uncooperative individuals as these and the problem presented to society by their existence. Why, then, did they sound so surprised and affronted at discovering that just the same problem afflicted the training wing?

This cool reply did not satisfy the complainants—they wanted such men to be punished, or otherwise dealt with. To this I replied that no doubt the complainants themselves had neurotic symptoms, or they would not be in hospital; why should their disabilities be treated in one way and the disabilities of the 80 per cent be treated in another? After all, the problem of the '80 per cent' was not new; in civil life magistrates, probation officers, social workers, the Church, and statesmen had all attempted to deal with it, some of them by discipline and punishment. The '80 per cent', however, were still with us; was it not possible that the nature of the problem had not yet been fully elucidated and that they (the complainants) were attempting to rush in with a cure before the disease had been diagnosed? The problem, I said, appeared to be one that not only concerned the training wing, or even the Army alone, but had the widest possible implications for society at large. I suggested that they should study it and come forward with fresh proposals when they felt they were beginning to see daylight.

It is worth remarking at this point that my determination not to attempt solution of any problem until its borders had become clearly defined helped to produce, after a vivid and healthy impatience, a real belief that the unit was meant to tackle its job with scientific seriousness. One critic expostulated that surely such a system of patient observation would be exceedingly slow in producing results, if indeed it produced results at all. He was answered by reminding him that only a few days previously the critic himself had spontaneously remarked that military discipline and bearing of the training wing had improved out of all recognition within the short period of one month.

The second example illustrates the development of an idea from the stage of rather wild, neurotic impulses to practical common-sense activity.

By far the largest group of men proposed the formation of a dancing class. Despite the veneer of a desire to test my sincerity in promising facilities for group activity, the pathetic sense of inferiority towards women that underlay this proposal, by men taking no part in fighting, was only too obvious. They were told to produce concrete proposals. The steps by which this was done need not detain us; in the end the class was held during hours usually taken up by an evening entertainment; it was confined, by the volition of the men themselves, only to those who had no knowledge at all of dancing and the instruction was done by ATS staff. In short, a proposal, which had started as a quite impractical idea, quite contrary to any apparently serious military aim, or sense of social responsibility to the nation at war, ended by being an inoffensive and serious study carried out at the end of a day's work. Furthermore, the men concerned had had to approach the Commanding Officer, the ATS officers, and the ATS, as a matter of discipline in the first place and social courtesy in the second.

In the meantime, the 12.10 parades had developed very fast into business-like, lively, and constructive meetings, and that in spite of the fact that the wing was now receiving heavy reinforcements of patients new to the organization, as well as losing others who had been discharged from hospital, often when they had become very useful.

Within a month of the inception of the scheme big changes had taken place. Whereas at first it almost seemed difficult to find ways of employing the men, at the end of the month it was difficult to find time for the work they wanted to do. Groups had already begun to operate well outside what were ordinarily considered parade hours; absence without leave was for a considerable period non-existent, and over the whole period there was only one case; patients not in the training wing became anxious to come over to it; and despite the changing population, the wing had an unmistakable *esprit de corps*, which showed itself in details such as the smartness with which men came to attention when officers entered the room at the 12.10 meetings. The relationship of the men to the officers was friendly and co-operative; they were eager to enlist the officers' sympathy in concerts and other activities which they were arranging. There was a subtle but unmistakable sense that the officers and men alike were engaged on a worth-while and important task, even though the men had not yet grasped quite fully the nature of the task on which they were engaged. The atmosphere was not unlike that seen in a unit of an army under the command of a general in whom they have confidence, even though they cannot know his plans.

COMMENT

It is not possible to draw many conclusions from an experiment lasting, in all, six weeks. Some problems that arose could not be fully explored in the time; others could not be openly discussed while the war was still in progress.

It was evident that the 12.10 meetings were increasingly concerned with the expression, on the part of the men, of their ability to make contact with reality and to regulate their relationships with others, and with their tasks, efficiently. The need for organization of seminars for group therapy had become clear, and the foundation of their commencement appeared to be firmly laid.

The whole concept of the 'occupation' of the training wing as a study of, and a training in, the management of interpersonal relationships within a group seemed to be amply justified as a therapeutic approach. Anyone with a knowledge of good fighting regiments in a theatre of war would have been struck by certain similarities in outlook in the men of such a unit and the men of the training wing. In these respects the attempt could be regarded as helpful; but there were also lessons to be learnt.

Some of these raised serious doubts about the suitability of a hospital milieu for psychotherapy. It was possible to envisage an organization that would be more fitly described as a psychiatric training unit; and, indeed, some work had been done in the elaboration of an establishment and a *modus operandi* of such a unit. With regard to the psychiatrist, also, there was room for some readjustment of outlook. If group therapy is to succeed it appears necessary that he should have the outlook, and the sort of intuitive sympathetic flair, of the good unit commander. Otherwise there will always be a lingering suspicion that some combatant officers are better psychiatrists, and achieve better results, than those who have devoted themselves to the narrow paths of individual interview.

Finally, attention may be drawn again to the fact that society, like the individual, may not want to deal with its distresses by psychological means until driven to do so by a realization that some at least of these distresses are psychological in origin. The community represented by the training wing had to learn this fact before the full force of its energy could be released in self-cure. What applied to the small community of the training wing may well apply to the community at large; and further insight may be needed before whole-hearted backing can be obtained for those who attempt in this way to deal with deep-seated springs of national morale.

APPLICATION OF GROUP THERAPY IN A SMALL WARD (J. R.)

An experiment in the application of group therapy, in the newer sense, to patients in a ward of 14-16 beds was made in the hospital division of the same institution. Each patient had an initial interview with the psychiatrist in which a personal history was taken in the usual way; thereafter there were group discussions every morning before the hour's 'route march'; and after it, as the patients returned to the ward, they could call in at the psychiatrist's room to discuss privately the topic of the group discussion, which had usually been the subject of conversation of the route march, and their personal feelings about it.

The therapeutic talks centred on their personal difficulties in putting the welfare of the group in the first place during their membership of the group. The topics of the group discussion included the following:

(a) Since residence in this ward is temporary, some going into the training wing and others coming from the admission ward to take their place, how is this changing situation to be met? We—the distinction between physician and patient, officer and other ranks, was another special topic—should have to accommodate ourselves to people entering our group to whom our attitude to our ward (it was always referred to as 'our ward') meant nothing at all; either we could regard them as outsiders or as imperfectly accommodated insiders. So, too, with those who 'went out' into the training wing: they could not expect to retain the ward-group attitude indefinitely, nor could they expect to include the much larger training wing in their ward-group; they would have to find their place in the new groupings and allow their ward experience to be but a memory, but it was to be hoped a helpful memory.

Then there was the further point whether those in the training wing should come back to the daily group discussions, the question being not what they would get out of them (there seemed little doubt they were among the most interesting experiences we had ever had) but whether, coming from another group-formation, or having lost their ward contact, they might not prove a distraction to those who were finding their feet in the ward-group.

(b) How far were the differences of rank acquired 'outside' to determine the behaviour of the members of the group to one another while in the ward? Would an attempt at equality work? Or would it be better, while not forgetting the rank acquired outside, to consider what equivalents of rank emerge when in the ward, and, if so, the basis of these equivalents?

(c) What makes for discontent in the ward? Is it something peculiar to the war, and any ward, or to any association of people?

(d) What makes for content and happiness in the ward? Is it the exercise of individual initiative having for its sole criterion the free expression of the person's own private enterprises, or does that come only after recognition of what the ward needs from the individual? Is there a fundamental incompatability between these two points of view, and, if so, does it apply to all or only some members? If to only some, what causes it to appear in these, and is it a characteristic they carry through in their lives all the time or is it stronger at some times than at others? If it varies, can the ward diminish it without being oppressive to those individuals so endowed?

The effect of this approach to the problem of neurosis was

considerable. There was a readiness, and at times an eager-ness, to discuss both in public and in private the social im-plications of personality problems. The neurotic is commonly regarded as being self-centred and averse from co-operative endeavour; but perhaps this is because he is seldom put in an environment in which *every* member is on the same footing as regards interpersonal relationships.

The experiment was interrupted by posting of personnel, so I cannot give clinical or statistical results; but it seemed to show that it is possible for a clinician to turn attention to the structure of a group and to the forces operating in that structure without losing touch with his patients and, further, that anxiety may be raised either inside or outside the group if this approach is made.

CONCLUSIONS

We are now in a better position to define the 'good group spirit' that has been our aim.

It is as hard to define as is the concept of good health in an individual; but some of its qualities appear to be associated with:

(a) A common purpose, whether that be overcoming an enemy or defending and fostering an ideal or a creative construction in the field of social relationships or in physical amenities.

(b) Common recognition by members of the group of the 'boundaries' of the group and their position and function in relation to those of larger units or groups.

(c) The capacity to absorb new members, and to lose

members without fear of losing group individuality—*i.e.* 'group character' must be flexible.

(d) Freedom from internal sub-groups having rigid (*i.e.* exclusive) boundaries. If a sub-group is present it must not be centred on any of its members nor on itself—treating other members of the main group as if they did not belong within the main group barrier—and the value of the sub-group to the function of the main group must be generally recognized.

(e) Each individual member is valued for his contribution to the group and has free movement within it, his freedom of locomotion being limited only by the generally accepted conditions devised and imposed by the group.

(f) The group must have the capacity to face discontent within the group and must have means to cope with discontent.

(g) The minimum size of the group is three. Two members have personal relationships; with three or more there is a change of quality (interpersonal relationship).

These experiments in a rehabilitation wing of a military psychiatric neurosis hospital suggest the need for further examination of the structure of groups and the interplay of forces within the groups. Psychology and psychopathology have focused attention on the individual often to the exclusion of the social field of which he is a part. There is a useful future in the study of the interplay of individual and social psychology, viewed as equally important interacting elements.

Experiences in Groups

1

Early in 1948 the Professional Committee of the Tavistock Clinic asked me to take therapeutic groups, employing my own technique. Now, I had no means of knowing what the Committee meant by this, but it was evident that in their view I had 'taken' therapeutic groups before. I had, it was true, had experience of trying to persuade groups composed of patients to make the study of their tensions a group task, and I assumed the Committee meant that they were willing that I should do this again. It was disconcerting to find that the Committee seemed to believe that patients could be cured in such groups as these. It made me think at the outset that their expectations of what happened in groups of which I was a member were very different from mine. Indeed, the only cure of which I could speak with certainty was related to a comparatively minor symptom of my own—a belief that groups might take kindly to my efforts. However, I agreed; so, in due course, I would find myself sitting in a room with eight or nine other people—sometimes more, sometimes less—sometimes patients, sometimes not. When the members of the group were not patients, I often found myself in a peculiar quandary. I will describe what happens.

At the appointed time members of the group begin to arrive; individuals engage each other in conversation for a short time, and then, when a certain number has collected, a silence falls on the group. After a while desultory conversation breaks out again, and then another silence falls. It becomes clear to me that I am, in some sense, the focus of attention in the group. Furthermore, I am aware of feeling uneasily that I am expected to do something. At this point I confide my anxieties to the group, remarking that, however mistaken my attitude might be, I feel just this.

I soon find that my confidence is not very well received. Indeed, there is some indignation that I should express such feelings without seeming to appreciate that the group is entitled to expect something from me. I do not dispute this, but content myself with pointing out that clearly the group cannot be getting from me what they feel they are entitled to expect. I wonder what these expectations are, and what has aroused them.

The friendliness of the group, though sorely tested, enables them to give me some information. Most members have been told that I would 'take' the group; some say that I have a reputation for knowing a lot about groups; some feel that I ought to explain what we are going to do; some thought it was to be a kind of seminar, or perhaps a lecture. When I draw attention to the fact that these ideas seem to me to be based on hearsay, there seems to be a feeling that I am attempting to deny my eminence as a 'taker' of groups. I feel, and say, that it is evident that the group had certain good expectations and beliefs about myself, and are sadly disappointed to find they are not true. The group is persuaded that the expectations are true, and that my behaviour is provocatively and deliberately disappointing—as much as to say, I could behave differently if I wanted to, and am only behaving like this out of spite. I point out that it is hard for the group to admit that this could be my way of taking groups, or even that I should be allowed to take them in such a way.

At this point the conversation seems to me to indicate that the group has changed its purpose.

While waiting for the group to settle on its new course, it may be useful if I try to offer the reader some explanation of behaviour which may, by this time, puzzle him as much as it does the group. I would not, of course, dream of doing this in a group, but the reader is in a different position from that of the man or woman who has much more evidence to go upon than the written word. Several questions may have occurred to the reader. He may think that my attitude to the group is artificially naïve, and certainly egotistical. Why should a group be bothered by having to discuss irrelevant matters such as the personality, history, career, and so forth, of one individual? I cannot hope to give any kind of full answer to such questions, but will say provisionally that I do not consider that I forced the group to discuss myself, though I do agree that the group was forced to do so. However irrelevant it may appear to be to the purpose of the meeting, the preoccupation with my personality certainly seemed to me to obtrude itself, unwelcome though that might be to the group or to myself. I was simply stating what I thought was happening. Of course, it may be argued that I provoked this situation, and it has to be admitted that this is quite possible, although I do not think so. But even supposing my observations are correct, it may be wondered what useful purpose is served in making them. Here I can only say I do not know if any useful purpose is served in making them. Nor am I very sure about the nature of this kind of observation. It would be tempting, by analogy with psycho-analysis, to call them interpretations of group transference, but I think any psycho-analyst would agree with me that, before such a description could be justified, a great deal of evidence from groups would have to be evaluated. But at least I can plead that observations of this kind are made spontaneously and

naturally in everyday life, that we cannot avoid making
them, unconsciously if not consciously, and that it would
be very useful if we could feel that when we made observations of this kind they corresponded to facts. We are constantly affected by what we feel to be the attitude of a group
to ourselves, and are consciously or unconsciously swayed
by our idea of it. It will be seen at once that it does not
follow that one should blurt it out in the way I have so far
described myself as doing in the group. This, I confess, must
be regarded as peculiar, although if precedent were required,
we are all familiar with certain types of people, particularly
those who tend to feel persecuted, who behave in this
manner. Not a happy precedent, the reader will think, and
it will not be long before it is evident that the group thinks
so too. But it is necessary now to return to the group, whom
we left in the process of changing course.

The first thing that strikes us is the improvement that has
taken place in the atmosphere. Mr. X, who has a likeable
personality, has taken charge of the group, and is already
taking steps to repair the deplorable situation created by
myself. But I have given a mistaken impression if I seemed
to suggest that we can watch this group in detachment, for
Mr. X, who is anxious for the welfare of the group, quite
rightly turns his attention to the source of the trouble,
which, from his point of view, is myself. You can see that he
has a very good idea of tackling at once those elements in his
group which are destructive of morale and good fellowship.
He therefore aske me directly what my object is, and why I
cannot give a straightforward explanation of my behaviour.
I can only apologize, and say that, beyond feeling that the
statement that I want to study group tensions is probably
a very inadequate description of my motives, I can throw no
light on his problem; he has a good deal of sympathy from
the group when he turns from this very unsatisfactory reply

to question one or two others, who seem to be more co-operative and frank than myself. I think, however, I detect some unwillingness on the part of the group to follow his lead wholeheartedly. The dissidents seem to have reassured themselves that the Committee of the Tavistock Clinic must have had some good purpose in saying that I was to take the group; they give the impression that they are determined to believe that experience of a group taken by myself is valuable, in spite of their observations so far.

Nevertheless, Mr. X is having some success. Mr. Y tells him he is a Probation Officer, and has come to get a scientific knowledge of groups, which he feels would be of value to him. Mr. R, though not professionally concerned, has always had an interest in the scientific study of groups. Mr. X, Mr. Y, and Mr. R also give some details of their background, and explain why they feel a scientific study would help them.

But now difficulties appear to be arising. Other members of the group are not so forthcoming as Mr. Y and Mr. R. Furthermore, there seems to be some irritation with Mr. X for taking the lead at all. Replies become evasive, and it looks as if even the information that has been obtained was not really quite the information that was wanted. I begin to feel, as the conversation becomes more desultory, that I am again the focus of discontent. Without quite knowing why, I suggest that what the group really wants to know is my motives for being present, and, since these have not been discovered, they are not satisfied with any substitute.

It is clear that my interpretation is not welcome. One or two members want to know why I should take curiosity, which would seem to be valid without any further explanation, upon myself. The impression I receive is that very little importance is attached to the view I express as a possible explanation of what is going on. It seems to me either to be ignored, or to be taken as evidence of a warped outlook in

3

myself. To make matters worse, it is not at all clear to me
that my observation, however correct, is really the most
useful one to make at the moment. But I have made it, and
prepare to watch what follows.

I should explain that this bald description does not do
justice to the emotional state of the group at this point.
Mr. X seems harassed to find his initiative ill-received, and
the rest of group seem to be in varying stages of discomfort.
For my part, I have to confess that it is a reaction with which
I am familiar in every group of which I have been a member.
I cannot, therefore, dismiss it simply as a peculiarity of this
group. To me it is clear that whatever the group may think
about Mr. X, it has much more serious misgivings about myself. In particular, I suspect that my personality, and
especially my capacity for social relationships, and, therefore, my fitness for the role I am expected to fill, is in
question. In the group we are contemplating at the moment,
discontent with what is taking place, and particularly with
my part in producing it, has risen to such a pitch that even
the continued existence of the group becomes a matter of
doubt to me. For some uncomfortable moments I fear it will
all end by my having to explain to the Professional Committee that their project has broken down through the inability of the group to tolerate my behaviour. I suspect from
their demeanour that similar gloomy thoughts, differently
orientated, are passing through the minds of the rest of the
group.

In the tense atmosphere prevailing my own thoughts are
not wholly reassuring. For one thing, I have recent memories
of a group in which my exclusion had been openly advocated;
for another, it is quite common for me to experience a
situation in which the group, while saying nothing, simply
ignores my presence, and excludes me from the discussion
quite as effectively as if I were not there. On some occasions

of this kind of crisis, the reaction has taken the milder form of suggestions that I have already excluded myself from the group, and that I make things difficult by not participating. A reaction as mild as this is quite reassuring, but I cannot forget that when I first attempted to put such methods into operation the experiment was terminated by my removal in fact from my post. I should prefer to believe that on that occasion the dismissal was due to coincidental circumstances, but I remember that, even so, the patients with whom I was dealing had constantly warned me, on what grounds I did not know, that serious attempts were being made to sabotage the scheme. I have, therefore, every reason, in such a situation as I am describing, to believe that the discontent is real, and may easily lead to the disruption of the group.

But on this occasion my anxieties are relieved by a new turn of events. Mr. Q suggests that logical argument at this point would hardly be likely to elicit the information wanted, and, indeed, it is possible that I would rather not explain why I make such an interpretation, because it would run counter to any idea of leaving the group to experience the nature of group phenomena for itself. He argues that, after all, I must have good reason for taking the line I do. The tension in the group is immediately relaxed, and a far more friendly attitude towards myself becomes apparent. It is clear that the group has a high opinion of myself after all, and I begin to feel that I have been perhaps treating the group unfairly by not being more communicative. For a moment I am impelled to make amends by responding to this friendly change with some explanation of my behaviour. Then I check myself, as I realize that the group has simply gone back to its former mood of insisting that hearsay is fact; so, instead of this, I point out that the group now appears to me to be coaxing me to mend my ways and fall in with their wish that my behaviour should conform more to what is expected or familiar to them in other fields. I also remark that the group has, in essence, ignored what was said by Mr. Q. The emphasis has been shifted from what Mr. Q intended to only one part of what he said, namely, that, after all, I was likely to know what I was about. In other words, it has been difficult for an individual member to convey meanings to the group which are other than those which the group wishes to entertain.

This time the group really is annoyed, and it is necessary to explain that they have every right to be. It is perfectly clear that nobody ever explained to them what it meant to be in a group in which I was present. For that matter, nobody ever explained to me what it was like to be in a group in which all the individual members of this group were present. But I have to realize that the only person whose presence has so far been found to be disagreeable is myself, so that any complaints I may have have not the same validity as those of other members. To me it is more than ever clear that there is some quite surprising contradiction in the situation in which I find myself. I, too, have heard rumours about the value of my contribution to groups; I have done my best to find out just in what respect my contribution was so remarkable, but have failed to elicit any information. I can, therefore, easily sympathize with the group, who feel that they are entitled to expect something different from what, in fact, they are getting. I can quite see that my statements must appear to the group to be as inaccurate as views of one's own position in a given society usually are, and, furthermore, to have very little relevance or importance for anybody but myself. I feel, therefore, that I must try to present a broader view of the situation than I have done so far.

With this in view, I say that I think my interpretations are disturbing the group. Furthermore, that the group interprets my interpretations as a revelation of the nature of my personality. No doubt attempts are being made to consider that they are in some way descriptive of the mental life of the group, but such attempts are overshadowed by a suspicion that my interpretations, when interpreted, throw more light on myself than on anything else, and that what is then revealed is in marked contrast with any expectations that members of the group had before they came. This, I think, must be very disturbing, but quite apart from any point of this sort, we have to recognize that perhaps members of the group assume too easily that the label on the box is a good description of the contents.

We must recognize now that a crisis has been reached, in that members may well have discovered that membership of a group in which I am a member happens to be an experience that they do not wish to have. In that way we have to face frankly that members of our group may need to leave, in exactly the same way as a person might wish to leave a room which he had entered under a mistaken impression. I do not myself believe that this is quite a correct description, because, I remind the group, it was quite clear that in the beginning the group was most unwilling to entertain any idea that they had not properly satisfied themselves of the accuracy of hearsay reports about myself. In my view, therefore, those who felt that they had been misled by others, and now wished to withdraw, ought seriously to consider why they resisted so strongly any statements that seemed to question the validity of their belief in the value of my contributions to a group.

At this point it is necessary that I should say that I consider the emotional forces underlying this situation to be very powerful. I do not believe for a moment that the objective fact—namely, that I am merely one member of a group possessing some degree of specialized knowledge, and in that respect no different from any other member of the group—would be likely to be accepted. The forces opposed to this are far too strong. One external group—that is, the Clinic responsible for saying that I am to take a group—has given the seal of its authority to a myth of unknown dimensions; but apart from this, I am certain that the group is quite unable to face the emotional tensions within it without believing that it has some sort of God who is fully responsible for all that takes place. It has to be faced, therefore, that no matter what interpretations may be given, by myself or anybody else, the probability is that the group will reinterpret them to suit its own desires, exactly as we have just seen it do with the contribution of Mr. Q. It therefore becomes important to point out that the means of communication within the group are tenuous in the extreme, and quite uncertain in their action. Indeed, one might almost think that it would be less misleading if each individual member of the group spoke a language unknown to the remainder. There would then be less risk of assuming that we understood what any given individual said.

The group has now turned somewhat resentfully, but with more anxiety than resentment, to another member of the group. I get the impression that they are looking to him to be leader, but without any real conviction that he can be leader. This impression is strengthened because the man in question shows every desire to efface himself. The conversation becomes more and more desultory, and I feel that for most of the group the experience is becoming painful and uninteresting. A fresh thought occurs to me, so I pass it on.

I tell the group that it seems to me we are determined to have a leader, and that the leader we want seems to possess certain characteristics against which we match the characteristics of the different individuals we try out. Judging by our rejections, we seem to know perfectly well what we want. At the same time, it would be very difficult to say from our experience so far what these desirable characteristics are. Nor is it obvious why we should require a leader. The time of meeting of the group has been laid down, and really there seem to be no other decisions that the group has to make. One would imagine that a leader was required in order to give effective orders to the group, to implement moment-to-moment decisions; but, if this is so, what is there in our present situation that would make us think that a leader of this kind is required? It cannot be the external situation, for our material needs and our relationships with external groups are stable, and would not seem to indicate that any decisions will be required in the near future. Either the desire for a leader is some emotional survival operating uselessly in the group as archaism, or else there is some awareness of a situation, which we have not defined, which demands the presence of such a person.

If my description of what it is like to be in a group of which I am a member has been at all adequate, the reader will have experienced some misgivings, harboured some òbjections, and reserved many questions for further discussion. At the present stage I wish only to isolate two features of the group experience for inspection; one of these is the futility of the conversation in the group. Judged by ordinary standards of social intercourse, the performance of the group is almost devoid of intellectual content. Furthermore, if we note how assumptions pass unchallenged as statements of fact, and are accepted as such, it seems clear that critical judgment is almost entirely absent. To appreciate this point the reader must remember that he is able to read this account in tranquillity, with unfettered use of his judgment. This is not the situation in the group. Whatever it may appear to be on the surface, that situation is charged with emotions which exert a powerful, and frequently unobserved, influence on the individual. As a result, his emotions are stirred to the detriment of his judgment. The group accordingly will often wrestle with intellectual problems that, one believes, the individual could solve without difficulty in another situation—a belief that will later be seen to be illusory. One of the main objects of our study may well turn out to be precisely the phenomena that produce these perturbations of rational behaviour in the group—phenomena whose existence I have only been able to indicate by descriptions of facts that bear less relationship to the object of our study than the lines of a monochrome print do to the colours of a painting in which colour is the all-important quality.

The second feature to which I must allude is the nature of my own contribution. It would be satisfying if I could now give a logical account of my technique—the technique the Professional Committee, it will be remembered, wished me to employ—but I am persuaded that it would also be very inaccurate and misleading. I shall, in the course of the sections that follow, give as accurate a description as I can of what I say and do, but I propose also to indicate what groups think I say and do, and this not merely to illustrate the mental working of a group, but to provide as much material as possible for the reader to use in reaching his own conclusions. I will, however, emphasize one aspect of my interpretations of group behaviour which appears to the group, and probably to the reader, to be merely incidental to my personality, but which is, in fact, quite deliberate—the fact that the interpretations would seem to be concerned with matters of no importance to anyone but myself.

2

I ended the previous section by saying that my interpretations of group behaviour in terms of the group's attitude to myself must seem to be a contribution as impertinent as it was likely to be inaccurate. Criticisms of this feature of my behaviour in a group require careful investigation, and the sequel will show that to these criticisms I shall provide answers, not refutations. Let us first consider a few group situations.

As we sit round in a rough circle, the room softly lit by a single standard lamp, a woman patient in the group complains angrily:

> You (that is, the group) always say I am monopolizing, but if I don't talk you just sit there like dumb things. I'm fed up with the whole damn lot of you. And you (pointing to a man of twenty-six, who raises his eyebrows in a smoothly efficient affectation of surprise) are the worst of the lot. Why do you always sit there like a good little boy—never saying anything, but upsetting the group? Dr. Bion is the only one who is ever listened to here, and he never says anything helpful. All right, then, I'll shut up. Let's see what you do about it if I don't monopolize.

Now another one: the room is the same, but it is a sunlit evening in summer; a man is speaking:

This is what I complain about here. I asked a perfectly simple question. I said what I thought was happening because I don't agree with Dr. Bion. I said it would be interesting to know what other people thought, but do any of you reply? Not a bloody one. And you women are the worst of the lot—except Miss X. How can we get anywhere at all if people won't answer you? You smile when I say except Miss X, and I know what you're thinking, but you're wrong.

Here is another: a woman patient says:

Everyone seems to agree absolutely with what Dr. Bion has just said, but I said the same thing five minutes ago, and because it was only me no one took the slightest notice.

And yet another; a woman says:

Well, since nobody else is saying anything, I may as well mention my dream. I dreamed that I was on the seashore, and I was going to bathe. There were a lot of seagulls about. . . . There was a good deal more like that.
A member of the group: Do you mean that that is all you can remember?
Woman: Oh, no, no. But it's all really rather silly.

The group sits about glumly, and each individual seems to become rapt in his thoughts. All contact between members of the group appears to have broken.

Myself: What made you stop talking about your dream?
Woman: Well, nobody seemed very interested, and I only said it to start the ball rolling.

I will draw attention only to one aspect of these episodes.

The first woman patient said: You (the group) always say I am monopolizing. . . . In actual fact, only one person had said this, and that on only one occasion, but her reference was to the whole group, and clearly indicated that she thought the whole group always felt this about her. The man in the second example said: You smile when I say except Miss X, and I know what you're thinking. . . . In the third example the woman said: . . . because it was only me no one took the slightest notice. In the fourth example the woman felt that the group was not interested, and that she had better abandon her initiative. I have already pointed out above that anyone who has any contact with reality is always consciously or unconsciously forming an estimate of the attitude of his group towards himself. These examples taken from groups of patients show, if there is really any need for demonstrations, that the same kind of thing is going on in the patient group. For the time being I am ignoring obvious facts, such as that there is something in the speaker which colours his assessment of the situation in which he finds himself. Now, even if it is still maintained that the individual's view of the group attitude to himself is of no concern to anybody but himself, I hope that it is clear that this kind of assessment is as much a part of the mental life of the individual as is his assessment, shall we say, of the information brought to him by his sense of touch. Therefore, the way in which a man assesses the group attitude to himself is, in fact, an important object of study even if it leads us to nothing else.

But my last example, of a very common occurrence, shows that, in fact, the way in which men and women in a group make these assessments is a matter of great importance to the group, for on the judgments that individuals make depends the efflorescence or decay of the social life of the group.

What happens if I use this idea of group attitude to the

individual as a basis for interpretation? We have already
seen some of the reactions in the first section. In the examples
I gave, there could be seen, though I did not stress them, some
results of this sort of interpretation; but one common reaction I shall mention now. The group will tend to express
still further its preoccupation with myself, and then a point
seems to be reached where, for the time being, the curiosity
of the group is satisfied. This may take two or three sessions.
Then the group begins the thing all over again, but this time
with some other member of the group. What happens is that
another member is the object of the forces that were previously concentrated on myself. When I think enough
evidence has accumulated to convince the group, I say that I
think this has happened. One difficulty about doing this is
that the transition from a preoccupation with myself to a
preoccupation with another member of the group is marked
by a period during which the preoccupation with the other
member shows unmistakable signs of containing a continued
preoccupation with myself. I have depicted this situation in
the first section (p. 33), where I describe myself as giving an
interpretation that, in questioning others, the group is really
preoccupied with myself. I think that on that occasion I
would have been more accurate if I had interpreted the
emotional situation as a transition of the kind I have just
described.

Many people dispute the accuracy of these interpretations.
Even when the majority of members in the group have had
unmistakable evidence that their behaviour is being affected
by a conscious or unconscious estimate of the group attitude
to themselves, they will say they do not know what the rest
of the group thinks about them, and they do not believe that
anyone else does either. This objection to the accuracy of the
interpretations must be accepted, even if we modify it by
claiming that accuracy is a matter of degree; for it is a sign

of awareness that one element in the individual's automatic assessment of the attitude of the group towards himself is doubt. If an individual claims he has no doubt at all, one would really like to know why not. Are there occasions when the group attitude is utterly unmistakable? Or is the individual unable to tolerate ignorance about a matter in which it is essential to be accurate if his behaviour in a society is to be wise? In a sense, I would say that the individual in a group is profiting by his experience if at one and the same time he becomes more accurate in his appreciation of his position in the emotional field, and more capable of accepting it as a fact that even his increased accuracy falls lamentably short of his needs.

It may be thought that my admission destroys the foundations of any technique relying on this kind of interpretation; but it does not. The nature of the emotional experience of interpretation is clarified, but its inevitability as part of human mental life is unaltered, and so is its primacy as a method. That can only be attacked when it can be demonstrated that some other mental activity deals more accurately with matters of greater relevance to the study of the group.

Here is an example of a reaction where the accuracy of the interpretation is questioned; the reader may like to bear the preceding passages in mind when he considers the conclusions I draw from this and the associated examples.

For some time I have been giving interpretations which have been listened to civilly, but conversation has been becoming more and more desultory, and I begin to feel that my interventions are not wanted; I say so in the following terms: During the past half hour the group has been discussing the international situation, but I have been claiming that the conversation was demonstrating something about ourselves. Each time I have done this I have felt my contribution was jarring and unwelcome. Now I am sure I am the object of your hostility for persisting in this kind of contribution.

For a moment or two after I have spoken there is a silence, and then a man member of the group says very civilly that he has felt no hostility at all to my interpretations, and has not observed that anybody else has either. Two or three other members of the group agree with him. Furthermore, the statements are made with moderation, and in a perfectly friendly manner, except possibly for what one might think was an excusable annoyance at having to give a reassurance that ought to have been unnecessary. In some respects I might say again that I feel I am being treated like a child who is being patiently dealt with in spite of his tiresomeness. However, I do not propose to consider this point just now, but rather to take perfectly seriously the statement made by these members of the group who seem to me to represent the whole group very fairly in denying any feeling of hostility. I feel that a correct assessment of the situation demands that I accept it as a fact that all individuals in the group are perfectly sincere and accurate when they say they feel no hostility towards myself.

I recall another episode of a similar kind.

Besides myself, three men and four women are present in the group; a man and a woman are absent. One of the men says to a woman:

> How did your affair go last week?
> *The woman:* You mean my party? Oh, that went all right. Very well, really. Why?
> *The man:* Well, I was just wondering. You were rather bothered about it if you remember.
> *The woman* (rather listlessly): Oh, yes. I was really.
> After a slight pause the man starts again.
> *He says:* You don't seem to want to say very much about it.

She replies: Oh, yes, I do really, but nothing much happened. It really went all right.

Another woman now joins in and tries to carry the conversation further, as if she felt aware that it was faltering,
but in a minute or two she also gives up. There is a pause,
and then another woman comes forward with an experience
she had during the week. She starts off quite briskly, and then
comes to a stop. One or two members attempt to encourage
her by their questions, but I feel that even the questioners
seem to be oppressed by some preoccupation. The atmosphere of the group is heavy with fruitless effort. Nothing
could be clearer to me than the determination of the individuals to make the session what they would consider to
be a success. If only it were not for the two absentees, I think,
I believe this group would be going very well. I begin myself
to feel frustrated, and I remember how much the last two
or three sessions have been spoilt because one or more members of the group have been absent. Three of the people
present at this session have been absent at one or other of
the last two sessions. It seems too bad that the group should
be spoilt like this when all are prepared to do their best. I
begin to wonder whether the group approach to problems is
really worth while when it affords so much opportunity for
apathy and obstruction about which one can do nothing. In
spite of the effort that is being made, I cannot see that the
conversation is anything but a waste of time. I wish I could
think of some illuminating interpretation, but the material
is so poor that there is nothing I can pick up at all. Various
people in the group are beginning to look at me in a hopeless
sort of way, as much as to say that they have done all they
can—it is up to me now—and, indeed, I feel they are quite
right. I wonder if there would be any point in saying that
they feel like this about me, but dismiss this because there

seems to be no point in telling them what they must know already.

The pauses are getting longer, comments more and more futile, when it occurs to me that the feelings which I am experiencing myself—in particular, oppression by the apathy of the group and an urge to say something useful and illuminating—are precisely those which the others present seem to have. A group whose members cannot attend regularly must be apathetic and indifferent to the sufferings of the individual patient.

When I begin to wonder what I can say by way of interpretation I am brought up against a difficulty that will have already occurred to the reader: what is this group which is unsympathetic and hostile to our work? I must assume that it consists of these same people that I see struggling hard to do the work, but, as far as I am concerned at any rate, it also includes the two absentees. I am reminded of looking through a microscope at an overthick section; with one focus I see, not very clearly perhaps, but with sufficient distinctness, one picture. If I alter the focus very slightly I see another. Using this as an analogy for what I am doing mentally, I shall now have another look at this group, and will then describe the pattern that I see with the altered focus.

The picture of hard-working individuals striving to solve their psychological problems is displaced by a picture of a group mobilized to express its hostility and contempt for neurotic patients and for all who may wish to approach neurotic problems seriously. This group at the moment seems to me to be led by the two absentees, who are indicating that there are better ways of spending their time than by engaging in the sort of experience with which the group is familiar when I am a member of it. At a previous session this group was led by one of the members now absent.

As I say, I am inclined to think that the present leaders of this group are not in the room; they are the two absentees, who are felt not only to be contemptuous of the group, but also to be expressing that contempt in action. The members of that group who are present are followers. I wonder as I listened to the discussion if I can make more precise the facts that give me this impression.

At first, I must confess, I see little to confirm me in my suspicions, but then I notice that one of the men who is asking the questions is employing a peculiarly supercilious tone. His response to the answers he receives appears to me, if I keep my mental microscope at the same focus, to express polite incredulity. A woman in the corner examines her fingernails with an air of faint distaste. When a silence occurs it is broken by a woman who, under the former focus, seemed to be doing her best to keep the work of the group going, with an interjection which expresses clearly her dissociation from participation in an essentially stupid game.

I do not think I have succeeded very well in giving precision to my impressions, but I think I see my way to resolving the difficulty in which I found myself in the first example. On that occasion, it will be remembered, I felt quite positive that the group was hostile to myself and my interpretations, but I had not a shred of evidence with which to back my interpretation persuasively. Truth to tell, I found both experiences very disconcerting; it seemed as if my chosen method of investigation had broken down, and broken down in the most obvious kind of way. Anyone used to individual therapy might have foretold that a group of patients would deny an interpretation, and anyone could have foretold that the group would present a heaven-sent opportunity for denying it effectively. It occurs to me, however, that if a group affords splendid opportunities for evasion and denial, it should afford equally splendid oppor-

4

tunities for observation of the way in which these evasions and denials are effected. Before investigating this, I shall examine the two examples I have given with a view to formulating some hypothesis that will give form to the investigation.

It can be seen that what the individual says or does in a group illumines both his own personality and his view of the group; sometimes his contribution illumines one more than the other. Some contributions he is prepared to make as coming unmistakably from himself, but there are others which he would wish to make anonymously. If the group can provide means by which contributions can be made anonymously, then the foundations are laid for a successful system of evasion and denial, and in the first examples I gave it was possibly because the hostility of the individuals was being contributed to the group anonymously that each member could quite sincerely deny that he felt hostile. We shall have to examine the mental life of the group closely to see how the group provides a means for making these anonymous contributions. I shall postulate a group mentality as the pool to which the anonymous contributions are made, and through which the impulses and desires implicit in these contributions are gratified. Any contribution to this group mentality must enlist the support of, or be in conformity with, the other anonymous contributions of the group. I should expect the group mentality to be distinguished by a uniformity that contrasted with the diversity of thought in the mentality of the individuals who have contributed to its formation. I should expect that the group mentality, as I have postulated it, would be opposed to the avowed aims of the individual members of the group. If experience shows that this hypothesis fulfils a useful function, further characteristics of the group mentality may be added from clinical observation.

Here are some experiences that seem to me to be to the point.

The group consists of four women and four men, including myself. The ages of the patients are between thirty-five and forty. The prevailing atmosphere is one of good temper and helpfulness. The room is cheerfully lit by evening sunlight.

Mrs. X: I had a nasty turn last week. I was standing in a queue waiting for my turn to go to the cinema when I felt ever so queer. Really, I thought I should faint or something.

Mrs. Y: You're lucky to have been going to a cinema. If I thought I could go to a cinema I should feel I had nothing to complain of at all.

Mrs. Z: I know what Mrs. X means. I feel just like that myself, only I should have had to leave the queue.

Mr. A: Have you tried stooping down? That makes the blood come back to your head. I expect you were feeling faint.

Mrs. X: It's not really faint.

Mrs. Y: I always find it does a lot of good to try exercises. I don't know if that's what Mr. A means.

Mrs. Z: I think you have to use your will-power. That's what worries me—I haven't got any.

Mr. B: I had something similar happen to me last week, only I wasn't even standing in a queue. I was just sitting at home quietly when . . .

Mr. C: You were lucky to be sitting at home quietly. If I was able to do that I shouldn't consider I had anything to grumble about.

Mrs. Z: I can sit at home quietly all right, but it's never being able to get out anywhere that bothers me. If you can't sit at home why don't you go to a cinema or something?

After listening for some time to this sort of talk, it becomes clear to me that anybody in this group who suffers from a neurotic complaint is going to be advised to do something which the speaker knows from his own experience to be absolutely futile. Furthermore, it is clear that nobody has the least patience with any neurotic symptom. A suspicion grows in my mind, until it becomes a certainty, that there is no hope whatever of expecting co-operation from this group. I am led to ask myself what else I expected from my experience as an individual therapist. I have always been quite familiar with the idea of a patient as a person whose capacity for co-operation is very slight. Why, then, should I feel disconcerted or aggrieved when a group of patients demonstrates precisely this quality? It occurs to me that perhaps this very fact will afford me an opportunity for getting a hearing for a more analytical approach. I reflect that from the way in which the group is going on its motto might be: 'Vendors of quack nostrums unite.' No soon have I said this to myself than I realize that I am expressing my feeling, not of the group's disharmony, but of its unity. Furthermore, I very soon become aware that it is not accidentally that I have attributed this slogan to the group, for every attempt I make to get a hearing shows that I have a united group against me. The idea that neurotics cannot co-operate has to be modified.

I shall not multiply examples of teamwork as a characteristic of the group mentality, chiefly because I cannot, at present, find any method of describing it. I shall rely upon chance instances as they occur in the course of these papers to give the reader a better idea of what I mean, but I suspect that no real idea can be obtained outside a group itself. For the present I shall observe that in the group mentality the individual finds a means of expressing contributions which he wishes to make anonymously, and, at the same time, his greatest obstacle to the fulfilment of the aims he wishes to achieve by membership of the group.

It may be thought that there are many other obstacles to the fulfilment of the individual's aims in a group. I do not wish to pre-judge the matter, but for the time being I shall not attach very much importance to them. It is clear that when a group forms the individuals forming it hope to achieve some satisfaction from it. It is also clear that the first thing they are aware of is a sense of frustration produced by the presence of the group of which they are members. It may be argued that it is quite inevitable that a group must satisfy some desires and frustrate others, but I am inclined to think that difficulties that are inherent in a group situation, such, for example, as a lack of privacy which must follow from the fact that a group provides you with company, produce quite a different sort of problem from the kind of problem produced by the group mentality.

I have often mentioned the individual in the course of my discussions of the group, but in putting forward the concept of a group mentality I have described the individual, particularly in the episode in which the two absentees played a big part in the emotional orientation of the group, as being in some way opposed to the group mentality although a contributor to it. It is time now that I turned to discuss the individual, and in doing so I propose to take leave of the neurotic and his problems.

Aristotle said man is a political animal, and, in so far as I understand his Politics, I gather that he means by this that for a man to lead a full life the group is essential. I hold no brief for what has always seemed to me an extremely dreary work, but I think that this statement is one that psychiatrists cannot forget without danger of achieving an unbalanced view of their subject. The point that I wish to make is that the group is essential to the fulfilment of a man's mental life

—quite as essential to that as it is to the more obvious activities of economics and war. In the first group described above (pp. 29 *et seq.*), I could say that the group was essential to myself because I wished to have a group to study; presumably the other members could say the same; but even had I admitted this as the aim of the individual members, including myself—and it will be remembered that I did no such thing—I consider that group mental life is essential to the full life of the individual, quite apart from any temporary or specific need, and that satisfaction of this need has to be sought through membership of a group. Now, the point that emerges in all the groups from which I have been drawing examples is that the most prominent feeling which the group experiences is a feeling of frustration—a very unpleasant surprise to the individual who comes seeking gratification. The resentment produced by this may, of course, be due to a naïve inability to understand the point that I made above, that it is the nature of a group to deny some desires in satisfying others, but I suspect that most resentment is caused through the expression in a group of impulses which individuals wish to satisfy anonymously, and the frustration produced in the individual by the consequences to himself that follow from this satisfaction. In other words, it is in this area, which I have temporarily demarcated as the group mentality, that I propose to look for the causes of the group's failure to afford the individual a full life. The situation will be perceived to be paradoxical and contradictory, but I do not propose to make any attempt to resolve these contradictions just now. I shall assume that the group is potentially capable of providing the individual with the gratification of a number of needs of his mental life which can only be provided by a group. I am excluding, obviously, the satisfactions of his mental life which can be obtained in solitude, and, less obviously, the satisfactions which can be obtained within his family. The power of the group to fulfil the needs of the individual is, I suggest, challenged by the group mentality. The group meets this challenge by the elaboration of a characteristic culture of the group. I employ the phrase 'culture of the group' in an extremely loose manner; I include in it the structure which the group achieves at any given moment, the occupations it pursues, and the organization it adopts. I will refer now to my speculations (p. 39) about the motives underlying the group's insistence on a leader. I said then that it would seem to be, in the situation I was describing, either an emotional survival operating uselessly, or else the response to some demand created by the awareness of a situation that we had not then defined. The attempt on that occasion to construct the group so that it consisted of a leader and his followers, above whom he towered supremely, is a very good example of the kind of thing I am meaning to include under the word culture. If we assume that the undefined situation is the group mentality of which I have been speaking, and I think there was good reason to assume that, then the group was attempting to meet the challenge presented to its capacity to fulfil the individual's need by this simple culture of leader and followers. It will be seen that, in the scheme I am now putting forward, the group can be regarded as an interplay between individual needs, group mentality, and culture. To illustrate what I mean by this triad, here is another episode taken from a group.

For a period of three or four weeks in a patient group I was in very bad odour—my contributions were ignored, the usual response being a polite silence, and then a continuation of the conversation which, as far as I could see, showed no sign of having been deflected by any comments of my own. Then suddenly a patient began to display what the group felt to be symptoms of madness, making statements that appeared to be the products of hallucination. Instantaneously I found I had been readmitted to the group. I was the good leader, master of the situation, fully capable of dealing with a crisis of this nature—in short, so outstandingly the right man for the job that it would have been presumption for any other member of the group to attempt to take any helpful initiative. The speed with which consternation was changed into bland complacency had to be seen to be believed. Before the patient began to alarm the group my interpretations might have been oracular pronouncements for all the ceremonious silence with which they were received; but they were the pronouncements of an oracle in decay—nobody would dream of considering their content as worthy of note. After the group had become alarmed I was the centre of a cult in its full power. Looked at from the point of view of an ordinary man attempting to do a serious job, neither situation was satisfactory. A group structure in which one member is a god, either established or discredited, has a very limited usefulness. The culture of the group in this instance might almost be described as a miniature theocracy. I do not attach importance to this phrase as a description, except in so far as it helps to define what on that occasion I would have meant by culture. Having done that, the proper employment of my hypothesis of individual, group mentality, and culture, requires an attempt to define the qualities of the other two components in the triad. Before the turning-point, the group mentality had been of such a nature that the needs of the individual were being successfully denied by the provision of a good friendly relationship between the patients, and a hostile and sceptical attitude towards myself. The group mentality operated very hardly upon this particular patient, for reasons into which it is unnecessary to go. It was possible on this occasion, by exhibiting something of the culture of the group, to effect a change in the group without elucidating either the group mentality or the effect upon the individual that the group mentality was having. The group changed and became very like school-children in the latency period in its outlook and behaviour. The seriously disturbed patient, outwardly at least, ceased to be disturbed. Individuals then attempted again to state their cases, but put forward only such problems as were of a trivial or painless nature. I was then able to suggest that the group had adopted a cultural pattern analagous to that of the playground, and that while this must be presumed to be coping fairly adequately with some of the difficulties of the group—I meant coping with the group mentality but did not say so—it was a culture which only permitted of the broaching of the kind of problem one might well expect a school-child to help with. The group again changed, and became one in which all members, including myself, seemed to be more or less on a level. At the same time a woman mentioned for the first time in six months quite serious marital difficulties that were troubling her.

These examples, I hope, give some idea of what I mean by culture, and also some idea of what I consider to be the need to attempt to elucidate, if possible, two of the three components in the triad.

My attempt to simplify, by means of the concepts I have adumbrated, will prove to be very misleading unless the reader bears in mind that the group situation is mostly perplexing and confused; operations of what I have called the group mentality, or of the group culture, only occasionally emerge in any strikingly clear way. Furthermore, the fact that one is involved in the emotional situation oneself makes clear-headedness difficult. There are times, such as the occasion I described when two members of the group were absent, when it is clear that the individuals are struggling against the apathy of the group. On that occasion I attributed behaviour to the group on the strength of the behaviour of one or two individuals in it. There is nothing out of the ordinary about this: a child is told that he or she is bringing disgrace upon the school, because it is expected that the behaviour of one will be interpreted as the behaviour of all; Germans are told that they are responsible for the behaviour of the Nazi government; silence, it is said, gives consent. Nobody is very happy about insisting on collective responsibility in this way, but I shall assume, nevertheless, that unless a group actively disavows its leader it is, in fact, following him. In short, I shall insist that I am quite justified in saying that the group feels such and such when, in fact, perhaps only one or two people would seem to provide by their behaviour warrant for such a statement, if, at the time of behaving like this, the group show no outward sign of repudiating the lead they are given. I dare say it will be possible to base belief in the complicity of the group on something more convincing than negative evidence, but for the time being I regard negative evidence as good enough.

3

In previous sections I explained the contribution I make in a group. I said that the emotional situation is nearly always tense and confused, so that it is not easy for the psychiatrist, who must necessarily be a part of the group, to tell what is going on. Feelings of frustration are common, boredom is acute, and often relief is provided only by outbursts of exasperation between members of the group. When an interpretation I give clarifies a situation that has been obscure for weeks there follows immediately a further period of obscurity which lasts as long again.

I probe this confusing situation by considering what position in the emotions of the group I myself occupy at any given moment, and I like to observe, at least for my own satisfaction, the sort of leadership that is being exercised by others in the group. I have suggested that it helped to elucidate the tensions of the group to suppose the existence of a group mentality. This term I use to describe what I believe to be the unanimous expression of the will of the group, an expression of will to which individuals contribute anonymously. I said that I thought this phenomenon in the mental life of the group caused difficulties to the individual in the pursuit of his aims. My third and last postulate was of a group culture, a term I used to describe those aspects of the be-

haviour of the group which seemed to be born of the conflict between group mentality and the desires of the individual. I gave some examples, as an illustration in concrete
terms of what I meant, of the experiences that had led me
to put forward these concepts..

In making interpretation to the group I avoid terms such
as group mentality; the terms used should be as simple and
precise as possible. Thus, I may say, speaking of what I call
group mentality: I think the group has got together during
the last five minutes in order to make anyone uncomfortable
who says or does anything to help me to give further interpretations. I should then describe facts that showed how the
group had done this and that had made me think that the
group had been working together as a team, even though I
may not have been able to detect how this team-work had
been achieved. If I thought I had some evidence of how it
had been achieved I would give it.

Or I might say, speaking of what I call group culture, we
are now behaving as if we were equals, grown men and
women, discussing the problem together freely, with toler-
ance for differences of opinion and without concern about a
'right' to express a point of view.

Or, speaking of the individual, I might say: Mr. X is having
difficulty, because he wants a problem of his dealt with, but
feels he is going to get into trouble with the rest of the group
if he perseveres in his attempt.

I have given this last example to show that the situation
could equally have been described in terms of group mentality, as in the first example. This is not a matter of importance by itself, but the psychiatrist must decide what
description best clarifies the situation for him, and then in
what terms he should describe it for the group.

I shall spend no more time on the way in which interpretations should be phrased; it is important, but I do not

think it can easily be communicated in a book. I will assume, therefore, that the reader understands that the situation should be described in concrete terms and the information given as fully and precisely as possible, without mention of the theoretical concepts on which the psychiatrist's own views have been based.

How did the use of these three concepts, group mentality, group culture, and individual, as interdependent phenomena, work in practice? Not very well; I found that the group reacted in a tiresomely erratic manner. I was able to give interpretations of the kind I have sketched out, and every now and then the reaction that followed could be explained as a logical development from the interpretation that I had given, but there were confusing exceptions. The group changed in ways that left me stranded and not able to apply my theories in any way that convinced me. Either I felt that they were inapplicable or, alternatively, that they illuminated some aspect of the situation that was of no significance.

I wish I could give concrete examples, but I cannot record what was actually said, and, in any case, the thing that knocked holes in my theories was not words used, but the emotion accompanying them. I shall, therefore, resort to an avowedly subjective account.

I have said that the effect of interpretation was erratic; however, after a time I thought that some patterns of behaviour were recurring and, in particular, one that went like this: two members of the group would become involved in a discussion; sometimes the exchange between the two could hardly be described but it would be evident that they were involved with each other, and that the group as a whole thought so too. On these occasions the group would sit in attentive silence—rather surprising behaviour in view of the neurotic's impatience of any activity that does not centre on his own problem. Whenever two people begin to have this kind of relationship in the group—whether these two are man and woman, man and man, or woman and woman—it seems to be a basic assumption, held both by the group and the pair concerned, that the relationship is a sexual one. It is as if there could be no possible reason for two people's coming together except sex. The group tolerates this situation, and, although knowing smiles are interchanged, the group seems prepared to allow the pair to continue their exchange indefinitely. There are exceptions, but they are not so numerous as one would imagine, considering the other individuals in the group have a good deal that they would like to say.

Now, it is clear that two people in a group can be meeting together for any number of purposes other than those of sex; there must, therefore, be considerable conflict between the desire of the pair to pursue the aim they have consciously in mind, and the emotions derived from the basic assumption that two people can be met together for only one purpose, and that a sexual one.

In due course the pair fall silent, and, if they are asked why, can find ready to hand many good reasons in reply—they do not want to monopolize; they had said all they had to say. I do not deny the validity of these explanations, but I would add another, and that is that the awareness that their contact does not conform to the basic assumption of the group, or, alternatively, conforms to the basic assumption of the group but does not conform to other views of what is proper behaviour in public.

Anyone who has employed a technique of investigation that depends on the presence of two people, and psychoanalysis is such a technique, can be regarded, not only as taking part in the investigation of one mind by another, but also as investigating the mentality not of a group but of a pair. If my observation of the basic assumption of the group is correct, it is not surprising that such an investigation seems to demonstrate sex as occupying a central position with other emotions as more or less secondary.

If the basic assumption about the pair is that they meet together for purposes of sex, what is the basic assumption in a group about people who meet together in a group? The basic assumption is that people come together as a group for purposes of preserving the group. It is common for discussions to become tiresome through preoccupation with absent members as a danger to the coherence of the group, and with present members as virtuous for being present. Anyone unaccustomed to this kind of group would be surprised to find how long a group of supposedly intelligent people can go on talking round this very limited field as if the discussion were emotionally satisfying. There is no concern to make the group worth preserving and, indeed, protests about the way the group employs its time, or any proposed change of occupation, are regarded as irrelevant to the discussion of the feared disintegration of the group. Outside the group, and sometimes in it, individuals believe that the way a group spends its time may regulate the intensity with which people wish to be members of it, but in the group it takes some time before individuals cease to be dominated by the feeling that adherence to the group is an end in itself.

My second point is that the group seems to know only two techniques of self-preservation, fight or flight. The frequency with which a group, when it is working as a group, resorts to one or other of these two procedures, and these two procedures only, for dealing with all its problems, made me first suspect the possibility that a basic assumption exists about becoming a group. Clinical observation gives as much reason for saying that the basic assumption is that the group has met for fight-flight, as for saying it has met to preserve the group. The latter is a convenient hypothesis for explaining why the group, which shows itself intolerant of activities that are not forms of fight-flight, will, nevertheless, tolerate the formation of pairs. Reproduction is recognized as equal with fight-flight in the preservation of a group.

Preoccupation with fight-flight leads the group to ignore other activities, or, if it cannot do this, to suppress them or run away from them. The basic assumption in a group about a group conflicts as sharply with other views about what a group can do as the basic assumption about pairs conflicts with the other views about what activities are proper to pairs.

From the basic assumption about groups there springs a number of subsidiary assumptions, some of immediate importance. The individual feels that in a group the welfare of the individual is a matter of secondary consideration—the group comes first, in flight the individual is abandoned; the paramount need is for the group to survive—not the individual.

The basic assumption of the group conflicts very sharply with the idea of a group met together to do a creative job, especially with the idea of a group met together to deal with the psychological difficulties of its members. There will be a feeling that the welfare of the individual does not matter so long as the group continues, and there will be a feeling that any method of dealing with neurosis that is neither fighting neurosis nor running away from the owner of it is either non-existent or directly opposed to the good of the group; a method like my own is not recognized as proper to either of the basic techniques of the group.

We all live in groups, and have plenty of experience, however unconscious, of what that means. It is, therefore, not surprising that critics of my attempts to use groups feel that it must be either unkind to the individual or a method of escape from his problems. It is assumed that if the human being as a gregarious animal chooses a group he does so to fight or run away from something.

The existence of such a basic assumption helps to explain why groups show that I, who am felt to be pre-eminent as the leader of the group, am also felt to be shirking the job. The kind of leadership that is recognized as appropriate is the leadership of the man who mobilizes the group to attack somebody, or alternatively to lead it in flight. In this context I may mention that when with Dr. Rickman[1] I tried an experiment in the treatment of troops at Northfield Military Hospital it was assumed either that we were trying to get troops into battle, or alternatively, that we were concerned to help a lot of scrimshankers to go on scrimshanking. The idea that treatment was contemplated was regarded as an elaborate, but easily penetrable deception. We learned that leaders who neither fight nor run away are not easily understood.

We have now reached this point: reactions to interpretations based on concepts of group mentality, group culture, and individual suggested that my theories were inadequate. Re-examination exposed the existence of basic assumptions about the object of pair relationships and group relationships. In the light of these basic assumptions I propose to modify the concepts of group mentality, thus:

Group mentality is the unanimous expression of the will of the group, contributed to by the individual in ways of which he is unaware, influencing him disagreeably whenever he thinks or behaves in a manner at variance with the basic assumptions. It is thus a machinery of intercommunication that is designed to ensure that group life is in accordance with the basic assumptions.

---

[1] See 'Pre-View', pp. 11-26.

5

Group culture is a function of the conflict between the individual's desires and the group mentality.

It will follow that the group culture will always show evidence of the underlying basic assumptions. To the two basic assumptions I have already described it is necessary to add one more. It is the basic assumption that the group has met together to obtain security from one individual on whom they depend.

The account given above (pp. 29-40) showed a group bewildered by the difference between what they expected of me and what they really found. There was anxiety that the group should proceed along well-established lines, e.g., those of a seminar or lecture. Although it was understood by each individual that we were met together to study groups and their tensions, in the group itself such an activity on my part did not appear to be comprehensible. When an alternative leader arose, before long he also was discarded, and the group returned to its allegiance to myself, though as unwilling as ever to recognize or accept the kind of lead that I gave. I described the group's desire to exclude me from membership. On another occasion, not dissimilar, members of the group had told me that attempts were being made to sabotage the group. In that section I said that the group required a leader to fulfil a function for which there was no scope, or at least a function for which I had not observed any scope.

My revised theories would have enabled me to understand the situation better than I did; my explanations and interpretations would have presented greater cohesion had I been able to relate them to the concepts I have just described.

First, the attempt to use the group as a seminar was intended to keep the group anchored to a sophisticated and rational level of behaviour, suitable to the fulfilment of the aims individuals wished to pursue; it was as if the group were aware that without some such attempt my procedure would lead to the obtrusion of a kind of group that was a hindrance rather than an aid to the consummation of the conscious wishes of the individual.

That attempt failing, there began to emerge the group that is, according to my theory, dominated by the basic assumption of unity for purposes of fight or flight.

With the emergence of this group the leadership that I was exercising became no longer recognizable as leadership. On the occasion of the warning against sabotage, had I been the leader that the group expected I would have understood the invitation to recognize the existence of an enemy—the first requisite of this kind of group. If you can only fight or run away you must find something to fight or run away from.

The substitute leader failed, but in this respect the group was peculiar. In my experience most groups, not only patient groups, find a substitute that satisfies them very well. It is usually a man or woman with marked paranoid trends; perhaps if the presence of an enemy is not immediately obvious to the group, the next best thing is for the group to choose a leader to whom it is.

A review of my past group experiences indicates that those experiences were not incompatible with my revised concepts. I shall now turn to the application of these theories in practice.

This is what happened with a group in which I had given interpretations showing how treatment had produced unpleasant feelings in members of the group. The effect of the interpretations had been to make members feel that I menaced the 'good' group. At one point my interpretation happened to hinge on remarks made by Miss Y. She listened to what I said and passed on smoothly as if I had not spoken at all. A few minutes later, when I gave another interpretation of the same kind, the same thing happened; a few minutes later, the same again. The group fell silent. At the moment when Miss Y had ignored my interpretation I was aware that the group had come together as a group; I had no doubt about this whatever. By the end of my third interpretation I was sure not only that the group had come together, but that it had done so to put an end to my interventions. I felt certain this determination received its embodiment in Mr. X, who had not said a word at any time. Mr. X was a man with strong feelings of hatred and marked fear of his aggressiveness. He talked only when the group was either a pairing group or a group met to satisfy the need for dependence. In both types of group, though he spoke, he spoke with diffidence, at least until he himself had developed. But in the group come together as a group he sat silent, and gave the impression of being deeply satisfied emotionally. That was the impression he gave at this point in my story.

During the silence I became aware that another patient in the group was experiencing a strong emotional satisfaction. In some respects he appeared to be of less importance than Mr. X, indeed subordinate to him. Mr. M, for so I shall call him, sat with his gaze fixed on Mr. X. From time to time his eyes would wander pensively to other members of the group as if he were watching to see if any member of the group wished to catch his eye. Mr. M speaks of his own difficulties rarely. He speaks as if he wishes to encourage the group by showing that no harm comes of being candid; yet if such is his aim he must fail, for surely the more percipient draw some other conclusion from the evidence that his contribution bears of polished and careful selection. On this occasion as his gaze rested on any individual as an invitation to speak his invitation passed unheeded.

Miss J began to give an account of some discomfort she had suffered at her work. When she had finished she briskly interposed a tentative interpretation of her behaviour. She then described some further episodes but finally gave up the attempt to ignore the stony hostility of the group and fell silent, remarking that she supposed she was too self-conscious to go on.

Miss H, who stepped into the breach next, only managed a few sentences before succumbing.

After the silence had continued for some time I remarked that individuals, Miss J and Miss H in particular, had tried to get on with treatment, as they felt it ought to be, by talking of their difficulties, partly because they felt that that was a useful thing to do to help myself and partly because they wanted to break up the hostile feeling in the group. The silence, I thought, might be regarded both as an expression of hostility of the group, and as an expression of the awareness of individuals that in the group as it was no creative work could be done.

The situation I have described was an emotional situation and is not easily conveyed by an account of the words used. It is this kind of episode that I am talking about when I speak of the group coming together as a group. When the group has come together in this way it has become something as real and as much a part of human life as a family, but it is in no way at all the same thing as a family. The leader of such a group is far removed from being the father of a family. In certain special emotional states, which I shall describe later, the leader approximates to a father, but in this kind of group any member of the group who displays parental qualities soon finds that he has none of the status, obligations, or privileges usually associated with a father or mother. Indeed in so far as I, as psychiatrist, am expected to display parental qualities, my own position in the group at this point becomes anomalous, and the expectation operates as an additional reason for my exclusion from the group—additional to the fact that my behaviour has already made the group combine against me as the enemy of the group. It requires the authority conferred by my position as psychiatrist to keep me in the picture at all when the basic assumption implies that a person whose primary concern is with the welfare of the individual is out of place.

Mr. X had no need to speak in this group; he was at one with the group, for the feelings about which he is most guilty, his destructive hatred, are feelings which are licensed by the basic assumption that the group has come together to fight or run away.

Mr. M played an interesting part; I found it necessary to devote careful attention to it. Before I could give an interpretation that would be comprehensible by the group I had to observe the expression on his face, and the order in which he called upon members of the group to participate. It was as if one were watching a silent film of a man conducting an orchestra: what sort of music did he wish to evoke? Mr. M's function was to keep hostility alive so that no one could fail to notice my impotence to effect any change whatever in the situation.

I kept drawing attention, in detail, to the emotional peculiarities of this situation. I was able to point out that individuals who produced difficulties of their own for help were ignored or sat upon, that attempts to be constructive were similarly dealt with, that there appeared to be subtle understanding between all members of the group, and that we worked together as a team in all that we did. I was able to show that various members of the group, for example, Mr. M, were communicating by a system of gestures, often of great subtlety, with the rest of the group. I added that there might be still other means of communication not yet recognized, perhaps because our powers of observation were still very limited.

It is not quite correct to say my interpretations were being ignored. There was something going on which made me feel that some of what I said was being taken in, but as far as outward appearance was concerned I might have been cut off from the rest of the group by a sheet of sound-proof plate glass. Certainly my interpretations did not make a scrap of difference to the behaviour of the group, which continued unresponsive for a good thirty minutes until time was up. As the reader will imagine, I had to ask myself why there was no response. The theories might again be at fault, or, alternatively, my interpretations incorrect. In fact, I felt that I was dealing with a situation similar to that which obtains in a psycho-analysis when the patient's lack of response is revealed at a subsequent session to have been very partial.

This, in fact, was what happened. At the next session the group was what I have described as the group met for purposes of pairing off. I would, however, prefer not to carry the description of this group any further, but to describe instead an occasion in another group which would serve better to make clear the change from one group culture to another. In the example I have given the interpretations appear to work their effect in the interval between meetings. I want to describe now a session in which the change was actually taking place. I shall choose an occasion when the change was from the fight-flight group.

The group had been frequently in the fight-flight state. On this occasion the group culture was proving extremely irksome to a number of individuals in the group, and at this point a man began a conversation with myself. It would not be fair to say that it was meaningless, because it had enough substance to demand a response. After a few sentences he broke off, as if he were aware that he was at the end of his resources in the art of talking without saying anything, and wished not to persevere to a point where this became too obvious. He was followed by a woman doing much the same. Both people behaved as if they were satisfied with the success of their venture. Each of them in turn repeated the procedure with two other members of the group. At this point others attempted to converse in much the same way as the pioneers, but it was noticeable that the conversations were no longer meaningless.

Had I seen this behaviour in a psycho-analysis I should have been inclined to think that the patient wished to obtain reassurance by establishing what he could feel to be a friendly contact with myself, without in any way divulging the nature of the anxiety against which he wished to be reassured.

In the group situation much the same interpretation could have been made, but, if this behaviour was to be accurately keyed to the emotions of that time and place, then the interpretation needed to be one that gave due weight to the social functions the individuals were performing. I accordingly interpreted their behaviour as a manipulation of the group; they were trying to break up the fight-flight culture by establishing pair relationships. As a first step in this procedure they got in touch with myself because experience had shown them that I was probably less likely to be so emotionally involved in the group situation as to be unable to react. It was then only a step to do the same thing with other members of the group, and from that point on it was only a matter of a few minutes before the group had changed over into the group met for purposes of pairing off. Once this had happened discussion of individual problems became possible again.

I have said that I wished to give this example to illustrate the change actually taking place, but I would like to continue with this episode to show what happens to individuals as the group passes from one group culture to another and back again.

As I said, this group had been suffering the frustrations of trying to live in a fight-flight culture. For a little while the pairing group seemed to afford welcome relief, but before long it became apparent that this sort of group had its disadvantages too. For one thing, my own role could not be very satisfactorily realized. In the fight-flight group the basic assumption of the group made it difficult for individuals to pay much attention to what I said or did. In the pairing group the basic assumption made it difficult for any individual to sustain a conversation with myself. It made conversation for any pair difficult, but the peculiar position occupied by the therapist exacerbates the difficulty. Those familiar with psycho-analytical theory will realize the kind of difficulties that obtrude as conversation goes on.

I mentioned that in the fight-flight culture the reactions of the group throw into prominence the individual with paranoid trends. Similar effects are obtained when the group passes to other cultures. Once one is aware of changes from a group culture with one basic assumption to a group culture with another basic assumption, it becomes possible to use these changes, to the benefit of one's clinical observation, in much the same kind of way as scientists in other fields are able to use changes of wavelength to obtain different photographic appearances of the object they wish to study.

In the two group cultures I have mentioned so far, difficulties are created for the psychiatrist because his job does not fit in easily with what is required from a leader of the group by the basic assumption. This makes the group unprepared to receive the contribution that the therapist makes. The therapist experiencing a lack of response from the group must, I think, bear this in mind as a factor that contributes its quota to the other factors making for his rejection. Should the therapist suspect that his high opinion of himself is shared by the group, he should ask himself if his leadership has begun to correspond with that demanded by the basic assumption of the group.

I wish now to consider the state I have described as the 'dependent' group culture.

The basic assumption in this group culture seems to be that an external object exists whose function it is to provide security for the immature organism. This means that one person is always felt to be in a position to supply the needs of the group, and the rest in a position in which their needs are supplied. When the group enters into this culture, and establishes it as an alternative to whichever one of the other two cultures it has been experiencing, much the same sort of relief is in evidence as I have already described in the change from the fight-flight group to the group met to pair. As the culture becomes established, individuals again begin to show their discomfort. One quite frequent phenomenon is the emergence of feelings of guilt about greed. A moment's thought will show that this might quite well be expected. The fight-flight culture or the culture of the group met for pairing do not, as far as the individual is concerned, represent survivals of an attitude beyond its proper term, although one might consider them to be primitive forms of group. But the group designed to perpetuate the state of dependence means for the individual that he is being greedy in demanding more than his fair term of parental care. There is, therefore, a quite sharp clash in this group between the basic assumption and the needs of the individual as an adult. In the other two group cultures the clash is between the basic assumption of what is required of the individual as an adult, and what the individual, as an adult, feels prepared to give. In this culture the feeling that the psychiatrist is some kind of parent is much more in evidence, and with this come the complications and difficulties that one would expect. Resentment at being in a dependent position is as much in evidence as relief. Sexual embarrassments are different from those displayed in the pairing group. Anger and jealousy are more easily expressed, but have not the massive quality and do not arouse the fear that they do in the fight-flight group. This, of course, is because of the basic assumption that a being exists who is there to see that no untoward events will follow the irresponsibilities of individuals. Hate in the fight-flight group is not accompanied by these reassurances, as the leader is felt to exist to express this and kindred emotions. Although there is relief because feelings can be expressed with greater freedom, there is conflict between the desire to do this and the desire to be mature.

When I spoke of the group that wished to see the session as a seminar, I said that one reason for this was an unconscious fear that unless the group were pegged to a mature structure the obtrusion of the kinds of group I have described would be facilitated and the ostensible aims of the individuals in joining the group thwarted instead of forwarded by coming together as a group. This impulse is expressed in the therapeutic group in the very fact of calling it a therapeutic group. It seems so rational that we should think of it as a therapeutic group, that we should assume that the psychiatrist is the leader, and that we should talk only about neurotic ailments, that it may not be observed that by thinking in this way, and behaving appropriately, we are attempting to peg the group to a mode of behaviour that will prevent the obtrusion of kinds of group that are feared.

4

In the preceding section I said that patients arrived with a preconception that serves very well as foundation for a structure intended to help the group to keep its behaviour pegged to a sophisticated level. The preconception is that the group consists of doctor and patients.

When men meet together, for example in a committee, rules of procedure are established and there is usually an agenda; the formality with which work is done varying with the group. In the groups in which I am psychiatrist I am the most obvious person, by virtue of my position, in whom to vest a right to establish rules of procedure. I take advantage of this position to establish no rules of procedure and to put forward no agenda.

From the moment when it becomes clear that I am doing this the group sets out to make good my omissions, and the intensity with which it does so shows that more is at stake than a passion for efficiency. The phenomena against which the group is guarding itself are none other than the group manifestations I described in the last section—the 'fight-flight group'; the 'pairing group'; and the 'dependent group'. It is as if the group were aware how easily and spontaneously it structures itself in a manner suitable for acting on these basic assumptions unless steps are taken to prevent it; just as a group of students may use the idea of a seminar or lecture on which to found a sophisticated structure, so the patient group has a basis for a structure ready to hand in the commonly accepted convention of neurotic disability as an illness and of therapists as 'doctors'.

THE DEPENDENT GROUP

The group concentrates at first on establishing this idea of doctor and patients as firmly as it can; it conforms to a strict discipline, imposed *ad hoc*, being careful to limit conversation severely to topics that are not important except in so far as they support the view that patients are talking to a doctor; thus would the group establish a sense that the situation is familiar and unchanging.

It is common at this point to see a group insisting that the doctor is the only person to be regarded, and at the same time showing by its behaviour that it does not believe that he, as a doctor, knows his job. If the psychiatrist himself feels impelled to help restore the sophisticated structure by claiming authority as psychiatrist, it shows that it is not the patient only who feels the need of a familiar situation. Maintenance of a sophisticated structure is associated with the feeling that the structure exists only precariously, and can easily be overset. When watching a group struggle with this problem, I am reminded of the warnings, frequent in recent years, that civilization itself was in danger. The problem of the leader seems always to be how to mobilize emotions associated with the basic assumptions without endangering the sophisticated structure that appears to secure to the individual his freedom to be an individual while remaining a member of the group. It was this balance of tensions which I previously described in terms of equilibrium between group mentality, group culture, and individual.

As I said, the doctor-patient foundation for a sophisticated structure soon shows its inadequacy, and one reason for this is that it is only a thin disguise for the dependent group, so that emotional reactions proper to this kind of basic group are immediately evoked, and the structure of sophistication sags badly.

Why should this matter? In the preceding section I drew attention to some of the discomforts of the situation, and we may now examine a few more. The dependent group, with its characteristic elevation of one person, makes difficulties for the ambitious, or indeed for anyone who wishes to get a hearing, because it means that in the eyes of the group, and of themselves, such people are in a position of rivalry with the leader. Benefit is felt no longer to come from the group, but from the leader of the group alone, with the result that individuals feel they are being treated only when talking to the leader of the group. This leads to a sense—the more unpleasant since it is associated with a feeling of asking too much and giving too little—that they are being cheated or starved. Relief obtained from the idea that the psychiatrist cares for each individual is unconvincing in a group that has been in existence for any time and knows that cure differs from a presumably transient experience of pleasant feelings. As each individual thinks he is being treated only while he is talking to the psychiatrist, the session appears to all members to achieve progress at a most uneconomic rate. This impression is only partly relieved by elucidations in detail of the manner in which the dependent structure of the group is clung to in spite of its discomforts.

The essential feature of the discomforts in this kind of group is that they arise precisely from the nature of the group itself, and this point should always be demonstrated.

When a dependent structure is prominent, it is quite common for an individual to arrive with an unpleasant mental experience about which he wishes to talk. The attitude of the group makes any consideration of his problem difficult, and the frustration of the patient's aims that this involves may appear a serious defect in this group technique, but again this must be set the fact that we are not concerned to give individual treatment in public, but to draw attention to the actual experiences of the group, and in this instance the way in which the group and individual deal with the individual. There is a further point: group patients often arrive with carefully prepared statements, and talk only when they think they can participate in a manner of their own choosing. If the psychiatrist reacts as if he were carrying out individual treatment in public he will soon become aware that he is working against the group and that the patient is working with it. If he has the strength of mind to avoid this pitfall, he will observe that the exasperation, at first sight so reasonable, of the patient whose pressing personal difficulty is being ignored, is dictated, not so much by the frustration of a legitimate aim, as by the exposure of difficulties the patient has *not* come to discuss, and in particular his characteristics as a group member, the characteristics of group membership, basic assumptions, and the rest of it. Thus a woman who starts off with a personal difficulty that she feels the psychiatrist could relieve, if he would respond by analysing her associations, finds, if the psychiatrist does not do this, that a totally unexpected situation has developed, and it will be surprising if the psychiatrist is not then able to demonstrate difficulties of the group, which will include difficulties of the patient in question, that the patient may think quite unimportant, but that turn out in the end not to be so. This of course is quite common in psycho-analysis— the topics discussed are not the ones the patient came to discuss. Nevertheless it is important to realize that the psycho-analyst can easily make a blunder in a group that he would never make in a psycho-analysis, by treating the group as if the procedure were psycho-analysis in public. The psychiatrist should be suspicious if he feels that he is dealing with the problem that the patient or the group thinks he should deal with. This point is critical; if the psychiatrist can manage boldly to use the group instead of spending his time more or less unconsciously apologizing for its presence, he will find that the immediate difficulties produced are more than neutralized by the advantages of a proper use of his medium.

In the dependent group, flight is confined to the group, fight to the psychiatrist; the impulse of the group is away from the hostile object; of the psychiatrist towards it. Apart from this, group emotions seem to be associated only with transitions from the dependent-group state of mind to one of the other two basic groups. The characteristics of this group are immaturity in individual relationships and inefficiency, except in the basic group, in group relationships—both conditions being countered to the best of the individual's ability by painstaking conscious communication. To grasp the full significance of these points it would be necessary to compare this state of affairs with the corresponding conditions in the other kinds of group.

Except in the leader, fearfulness becomes the supreme virtue of the individual in this kind of group. Participation in this emotional field means a heightened capacity, as soon as any member of the group experiences fear, for instantaneous flight. Such a state of affairs is very disagreeable to the individual, who, after all, retains full consciousness of his desires as a fully grown adult.

The group often structures itself as a dependent group in order to avoid emotional experiences peculiar to the pairing and fight-flight groups. In some respects the dependent group lends itself very well to do this, because, as I have suggested,

6

the group can restrict itself to the experience of flight, leaving
the analyst to experience, if he will, what it means to address
himself to the problems from which the group is running
away. This symbiotic relationship between the group and
myself—the psychiatrist—serves to protect members of the
group from experiencing certain aspects of group life for
which they do not feel prepared. They are thus left free to
make exercises in the development of sophisticated relationships with myself. I say 'with myself' because early experiences of the dependent group at any rate indicate that there
is a marked inability on the part of the individuals in the
group to believe that they can possibly learn anything of
value from each other.

From what I have said it should be clear that members of a
group in a dependent state of mind are finding that their experiences are unsatisfying. Anyhow, their mood contrasts
with that which they experience when, having thrown all
their cares on the leader, they sit back and wait for him to
solve all their problems. Thanks to interpretations I have
been able to give, they are not able to ascribe their immediate
disillusionment merely to my failure to do what a leader of
this kind of group is supposed to do. In fact, if the group
harboured any such idea, it could only be because I was failing completely to elucidate what was taking place. The point
is that this basic assumption, and the emotional field which
is its concomitant, produces its characteristic frustrations,
some more apparent to one patient, some to another.

When investigation of the dependent group has developed,
it becomes possible to observe the emergence of certain
characteristics that now demand attention. The group always
make it clear that they expect me to act with authority as
the leader of the group, and this responsibility I accept,
though not in the way the group expect. In the early stages
it seems sensible to think that this authority is based on the

idea that I am a doctor and they are patients, but there are features in the behaviour of the group whose emergence in the course of time shows that the situation is more complex. The insistence of the group that no one but myself has any right to command attention is matched by a firm sense of disappointment in what I do; an unshakable belief that they are justified in thinking I am qualified by training and experience to lead the group is matched by an almost equally unshakable indifference to everything I say.[1]

If I take account of the emotional atmosphere of the group —and it would require a considerable capacity for denial not to do so—it is clear that the group is not concerned to understand the point of what I say, but rather to make use only of such parts of my contribution as they can conveniently weld into what appears to be an already well-established *corpus* of belief. Gestures, tone of voice, manner, and appearance; and on occasions even the subject matter of what I say; none of it comes amiss, if it can be fitted into this system. The group is combining to establish a firm portrait of the object on which it can depend.

At first it is not easy to recognize the features of this portrait, but even so it is clear that they are not the features of a doctor. The same fate befalls any other member of the

---

[1] It has been erroneously said that my technique is based on the leaderless group technique used in the selection, in wartime. of candidates for training as officers for the British Army. This is not so; a memorandum I wrote in 1940 was the stimulus for an experiment, carried out by Dr. John Rickman at Wharncliffe Emergency Hospital, which subsequently became known as the Wharncliffe Experiment. The experience he gained there was used by him and myself as the starting-point for a further experiment at Northfield Military Hospital. The fame, or notoriety, achieved by this experiment gave currency to the name 'Northfield Experiment'. This name has since achieved respectability by being appropriated to activities more in keeping with the sober traditions of discipline and patriotism for which the British Army is justly famous.

group who is exalted in my place, with the result that individuals in the group, without exception, find that they influence the group in a manner capricious and only obscurely related to the thoughts that they strive to express. The endeavour that I myself make is to illuminate the obscurities of the situation in the group by clear thinking clearly expressed; it is at the best of times a considerable ambition, but in time it becomes clear that amongst other factors that go to make this a difficult aim to achieve is the hostility of the group to the aim, as an aim. The nature of this hostility can be best apprehended if it is considered as a hostility to all scientific method and therefore as hostility to any activity that might appear to be approaching this ideal. Complaints will be heard that my remarks are theoretical; that they are mere intellectualizations; that my manner lacks warmth; that I am too abstract. Study of the group over a period will show that, although there is no need to doubt the capacity of the individuals in the group for doing hard work, the group, as a group, is quite opposed to the idea that they are met for the purpose of doing work, and indeed react as if some important principle would be infringed if they were to work. I shall not enter into more detail on this point but perhaps, if the reader will turn back to some of my previous descriptions of behaviour in the group, he will recognize in the descriptions some of the traits I am describing (in particular, p. 39 and pp. 51-2). I shall now suggest that all facets of behaviour in the dependent group can be recognized as related if we suppose that in this group power is believed to flow not from science but from magic. One of the characteristics demanded of the leader of the group, then, is that he should either be a magician or behave like one. Silences in a dependent group are accordingly either expressions of determination to deny to the leader the material he requires for scientific investigation, and thereby to prevent developments that would appear to undermine the illusion of security derived from care at the hands of a magician, or expressions of worshipful devotion to the leader, as magician—an interpretation will often be followed by a silence that is far more a tribute of awe than a pause for thought.

When the group has reached this stage of development, the psychiatrist may think that he is dealing with 'resistances' in the ordinary sense of that term, but I believe that it is more fruitful to consider the group as a community that felt that a hostile attack was being made upon its religious beliefs. Indeed, it is quite common to find at this stage that references to religion are frequent. Sometimes the individual identifies himself with the investigator, sometimes with the investigated. If he identifies himself with the investigator, it is noticeable that he assumes a somewhat artificially self-assured air, as if to indicate either that he were investigating an interesting survival of the past or one of the well-known religions of the world, such as Buddhism or Christianity. This air is assumed in order to avoid realizing that he is investigating on the spot an emotionally vital 'religion', whose devotees surround him and are waiting to fall upon him. If the psychiatrist presses on vigorously with his investigation, he should have a lively sense of the hostility of the group and an emotional realization of the vitality of the phenomena with which he has to deal. He must be aware also that he should consider not only the *dogmata* of the cult, but all related phenomena, such as the demands it makes upon the lives of its devotees. Some of these can be witnessed in the group itself: the stifling of independent thought, the heresy-hunting, the rebellion this in its turn produces, the attempts to justify the imposed limitations by appeals to reason, or, at any rate, rationalization, and so forth. Other manifestations, however, become clear in the report that individuals give of their everyday life. For the 'devotees' of the group 'religion', rebellious or otherwise, remain 'devotees' also in their everyday life, and it is possible to show that some of their daily conflicts are arising from their attempt to reconcile the demands of everyday thinking and the demands of their membership of the group as a 'religious' community. The implications of this view of the group are great, and the more I see of this aspect of the dependent group, the more I am convinced that patients produce material in a steady stream to support the view that their membership of the dependent group, as a 'religious' sect, exerts a widespread influence on their mental lives when the group disperses as well as in the short period when they meet as a group.

I shall turn now to another problem.

THE HATRED OF LEARNING BY EXPERIENCE

If the group has to work constantly at maintaining a sophisticated structure, there must be a pull in the opposite direction towards one of the three basic structures, and it is important to view the group from that angle. Before doing so I will refer briefly to the need for employing a technique of constantly changing points of view. The psychiatrist must see the reverse as well as the obverse of every situation, if he can. He must employ a kind of psychological shift best illustrated by the analogy of this well-known diagram.

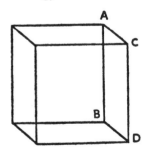

The observer can look at it so that he sees it as a box with the corner A B nearest to him; or he can view it as a box with the corner C D nearest to him. The total of lines observed remains the same, but a quite different view of the box is obtained. Similarly, in a group, the total of what is taking place remains the same, but a change of perspective can bring out quite different phenomena. The psychiatrist must not always wait for changes in the group before he describes what he sees. There are many times when he needs to point out that what he has just described has already been experienced by the group on some previous occasion, but then it was more easily observed in other terms, when, for example (to take the case of an individual), a patient had complained of considerable anxiety about 'fainting off'. Sometimes he had described the same phenomenon as 'becoming unconscious'. At a later group he was somewhat boastfully saying that, when things happened in the group which he did not like, he simply ignored them. It was possible to show him that he was describing exactly the same situation, this time in a mood of confidence, as he had on another occasion described with anxiety as 'fainting off'. His attitude to events in the group had altered with an alteration in the basic assumption of the group.

Neither analogy of obverse and reverse, nor yet the analogy of shift in perspective, really serves to cover the technique a psychiatrist should employ, so, to make my meaning clear, I shall use the analogy afforded by the principles of duality in mathematics. By these, a theorem that proves the relationship in space of points, lines, and planes appears equally to prove the relationship of its dual in terms of planes, lines, and points. In the group the psychiatrist should consider from time to time what is the 'dual' of any given emotional situation that he has observed. He should consider also whether the 'dual' of the situation he has just described has not already been experienced and described at some previous session.

Let us apply this now to the observation of the group: it will be remembered that I have described that after groups have assembled, but before they have become used to the technique, there is a pause while everybody 'waits for the group to begin'. It is quite common for someone to ask when the group begins. Now from one point of view the perfectly simple answer is that the group begins at 10.30, or whatever the hour is that has been appointed for the meeting, but a shift of point of view, admittedly of some magnitude, on my part, means that I am viewing group phenomena that do not 'begin'; the matters with which I am concerned continue, and evolve, but they do not 'begin'. In the work I do in the group, therefore, this question is not answered, although it can be seen that, if the group cares to invest me with leadership of a different kind from that which I propose to exercise, it can readily assume that it is my business to know when the group begins, or, for that matter, when it ends. There is no reason why one should not give the reply that is expected, so long as one is aware that the point is of some importance and involves a considerable change of role, though this point may not be apparent just now.

If, in a group, I have succeeded in demonstrating the struggle to maintain the sophisticated structure, I must also have succeeded in demonstrating its 'dual'. What follows is a description of the 'dual', though at first sight it may be difficult to realize its affinity with the attempt to preserve a sophisticated structure.

In every group it will be common at some time or another to find patients complaining that treatment is long; that they always forget what happened in the previous group; that they do not seem to have learnt anything; and that they do not see, not only what the interpretations have to do with their case, but what the emotional experiences to which I am trying to draw attention can matter to them. They also show, as in psycho-analysis, that they do not have much belief in their capacity for learning by experience—'What we learn from history is that we do not learn from history'.

Now all this, and more like it, really boils down to the hatred of a process of development. Even the complaint about time, which seems reasonable enough, is only to complain of one of the essentials of the process of development. There is a hatred of having to learn by experience at all, and lack of faith in the worth of such a kind of learning. A little experience of groups soon shows that this is not simply a negative attitude; the process of development is really being compared with some other state, the nature of which is not immediately apparent. The belief in this other state often shows itself in everyday life, perhaps most clearly in the schoolboy belief in the hero who never does any work and yet is always top of the form—the opposite of the 'swot', in fact.

In the group it becomes very clear that this longed-for alternative to the group procedure is really something like arriving fully equipped as an adult fitted by instinct to know without training or development exactly how to live and move and have his being in a group.

There is only one kind of group and one kind of man that approximates to this dream, and that is the basic group— the group dominated by one of the three basic assumptions, dependence, pairing, and flight or fight—and the man who is able to sink his identity in the herd.

I do not suggest for a moment that this ideal corresponds to reality, for, of course, the whole group-therapeutic experience shows that the group and the individuals in it are hopelessly committed to a developmental procedure, no matter what might have been the case with our remote ancestors.

My experience of groups, indeed, indicates that man is hopelessly committed to both states of affairs. In any group there can be seen the man who tries to identify himself wholeheartedly with the basic assumption, or wholeheartedly with the sophisticated outlook. If he identifies himself wholeheartedly with the basic assumption—with the herd, as it were—he feels persecuted by what he feels to be the arid intellectualism of the group and, in particular, of the interpretations. If he identifies himself, as far as he possibly can, with the purely intellectual outlook, he finds himself persecuted by internal objects, which, I suspect, are really a form of awareness of intimations of the emotional movements of the group of which he is a member; certainly some explanation of this kind would help to throw light on the individual's feeling that he was being persecuted by the group, both internally and externally.

In the group the patient feels he must try to co-operate. He discovers that his capacity for co-operation is emotionally most vital in the basic group, and that, in the pursuit of objectives that do not easily lend themselves to the techniques of the basic group, his ability to co-operate is dependent on a kind of give and take that is achieved with great difficulty compared with the swift emotional response that comes of acquiescence in the emotions of the basic group.

In the group the individual becomes aware of capacities that are only potential so long as he is in comparative isolation. The group, therefore, is more than the aggregate of individuals, because an individual in a group is more than an individual in isolation. Furthermore, the individual in a group is aware that the additional potentialities that then become activated by membership of the group are, many of them, best adapted for function in the basic group, that is to say, the group come together to act on the basic assumptions.

One of the problems of group therapy, then, lies in the fact that the group is often used to achieve a sense of vitality by total submergence in the group, or a sense of individual independence by total repudiation of the group, and that part of the individual's mental life, which is being incessantly stimulated and activated by his group, is his inalienable inheritance as a group animal.

It is this feature of group membership that gives rise to a feeling in the individual that he can never catch up with a course of events to which he is always, at any given moment, already committed. There is a matrix of thought which lies within the confines of the basic group, but not within the confines of the individual. There is also the individual's desire to feel that he is master of his fate, and to concentrate upon those aspects of his mental life which he can feel are most truly his own and originate within him. It is this desire that tends to make him more willing to observe phenomena that are related to that kind of group about which he can reasonably say that it 'begins', rather than to the kind of group in which the concept of 'beginning' has no place.

If the desire for security were all that influenced the individual, then the dependent group might suffice, but the individual needs more than security for himself and therefore needs other kinds of group. If the individual were prepared to suffer the pains of development, and all that that implies in efforts to learn, he might grow out of the dependent group. But the fact that he wishes, even with the impulses that are not satisfied in the dependent group, for a state in which, without undergoing the pains of growth, he could be fully equipped for group life, results in a pull towards a group structured for pairing or for fight-flight.

5

The emotional state proper to a basic assumption is not wholly pleasurable. As with the analyst in psycho-analysis, so with the group. In my technique with the group, the individual, supported by the group, tries to keep the goodness of the group isolated from its badness, and will maintain either that he feels 'bad' because of the group or that he feels 'good' because of it, but will not easily admit that certain agreeable emotional states called 'feeling better' are derived from the group of which he complains nor yet that certain unpleasant emotional experiences called 'feeling worse' are inseparable from membership of the group in whose goodness he would prefer for the moment to believe. In addition to the reasons commonly discoverable in psycho-analysis for this kind of behaviour, the individual in the group has reasons that derive directly from peculiarities of the emotional states associated with the basic assumptions, and it is these peculiarities that I shall now discuss. The investigation is provoked by the fact that the emotions associated with any basic assumption appear to be experienced by the individual in their entirety. My original description of a group acting on a basis assumption did not do justice to some features of the group behaviour that are now relevant. It might have been thought that the group makes a common assumption and that all else, including the emotional state associated with it, springs from this. This does not reflect my belief. On the contrary, I consider the emotional state to be in existence and the basic assumption to be deducible from it. As far as the group is concerned, the basic assumption is essentially a tacit assumption. Individuals behave as if they were aware of the assumption, and it is for this reason that the interpretation of the basic assumption carries conviction. It is a statement that gives meaning to the behaviour of the group as a whole, yet the assumption is not overtly expressed even when it is being acted on. We thus have a situation in which the individuals behave as if they were conscious, as individuals, of the basic assumption, but unconscious of it as members of the group. This is as it should be: the group has not a conscious; and it is not articulate; it is left to the individual to be both.

It is possible to talk of a feeling of security as existing in each of the emotional states associated with the three basic-assumption groups. Yet it is clear that the feeling of security experienced in the dependent group is really a feeling held in an indissoluble combination with the remaining feelings and ideas that compose the basic assumption of the dependent group, and it is therefore different from the feeling of security in both the fight-flight and pairing groups, which are similarly held in indissoluble combination with the remaining emotions and ideas proper to their respective groups. Thus the feeling of security derived from the dependent group is indissolubly linked with feelings of inadequacy and frustration, and is dependent on the attribution of omnipotence and omniscience to one member of the group. Since the psychiatrist cannot usually be manipulated into giving substance to beliefs in his omnipotence and omniscience, individuals will also show that their sense of security is qualified by the pressure of the group's demand on its individuals to be omniscient. Similarly in the fight-flight group, security is tempered by the demand of the group for courage and self-sacrifice; in short, the important thing is not so much any given feeling—for example, security—but the combination in which that feeling is held. Various feelings, not in themselves unpleasant, indeed greatly desired by the individual, cannot be experienced except fixed in combination with other less desired and often strongly disliked feelings, so the individual has to resort to splitting to isolate himself from the group and from his own essential 'groupishness'—his inalienable quality as a herd animal. The complaint that the individual cannot think in the group is often heard. He will try to feel secure in his membership of the group but will endeavour to split off the disliked feelings that are in combination with this desirable security; he will attribute the origin of these to some cause other than that very security he exacts—to some cause such as membership of a less important group, or some ephemeral external event, or to neurosis. Thus a deal of time has to be devoted to elucidation of the basic assumption from which emotional reinforcement is being derived, and then to the proof that the emotional experiences that patients often introduce into the discussion as symptoms are really derived from their being at one with other members of the emotionally reinforced group, and their conflict both with themselves and the group. The point that I wish to make is that participation in a basic assumption is not only unavoidable but involves a sharing of emotions which are, as far as psychological investigation can reveal them, discrete and separate one from another, but in fact only apparently so, and then only at that point in their history when they are manifest as psychological phenomena. The result is that to the psychologist there are not available any observations that can explain why, when one basic assumption is being acted on, the feelings associated with it are always linked with each other with the tenacity and exclusiveness, not more or less, that one would associate with chemical combinations.

It does not follow, of course, that this will always be so: it is conceivable that group technique might develop to a point where phenomena which are at present unrecognized will become perceptible. In the meantime, I wish to emphasize that it follows from what I have been saying that the individual's distress is idiopathic to the basic assumption that is being acted upon, that is to say, it arises from his conflict with the emotional state of the group and that part of himself which is concerned with participation in the group task of maintaining it.

The emotional state associated with each basic assumption excludes the emotional states proper to the other two basic assumptions, but it does not exclude the emotions proper to the sophisticated group. Hitherto I have said little about the sophisticated group, being content to describe the conflicts in a group as being between the individual and the basic group, and between the individual and himself as an upholder of, and participant in, the basic group. There is, however, a conflict between the group that is formed through cooperation between individuals at a sophisticated level—the sophisticated group—and the basic group, and in this respect the relationship between sophisticated and basic group differs from the relationship that obtains between the emotional states associated with the three basic assumptions. There is no direct conflict between basic assumptions, but only changes from one state to another, which are either smooth transitions or brought about through intervention of the sophisticated group. They do not conflict, they alternate; conflict arises only at the junction between the basic group and the sophisticated group.

Nevertheless, although the basic-assumption groups seem rather to alternate than to conflict with each other, the inter-

vention of the sophisticated group, through interference with
the alternation of the basic groups, seems to produce some of
the appearances and effects of conflict. In particular, the
emotional combinations associated with the basic assumptions that are not actively influencing the group's mental life
lie dormant, sometimes perhaps for considerable periods.
Thus when a group is pervaded by the emotions of the dependent group the emotional states of the fight-flight group
and pairing group are in abeyance. They are not manifest in
the sense that the emotions of the dependent group are manifest. In this respect there is a conflict between the sophisticated group, suffused by emotion from one basic assumption, and the other two basic assumptions. In this context it
is necessary to recognize that interpretations given by myself, if accepted, are themselves interpretations by the
sophisticated group. This immediately gives rise to certain
speculations. What is the difference between the form of
intervention that an interpretation represents and the other
interventions of the sophisticated group? If interventions by
the sophisticated group seem to produce some of the effects
or appearance of conflict between one basic assumption and
the others, does an interpretation also produce conflict? If
the interpretation does not produce conflict, what does it do?
For the time being I propose to ignore these questions and to
pass on to consider the fate of the potential emotional states
represented by the basic assumptions that are not at any
given moment being acted upon, and their relationship to the
sophisticated group.

The interventions of the sophisticated group are diverse,
but they all have this in common: they are expressions of a
recognition for the need to develop rather than to rely upon
the effcacy of magic; they are intended to cope with the basic
assumptions, and they mobilize the emotions of one basic
assumption in the attempt to cope with the emotions and

7

phenomena of another basic assumption. It is this that gives
the appearance of conflict between basic assumptions that I
have already mentioned. One result of this operation of the
sophisticated group is that the more sophisticated a group
becomes and the more it manages to maintain a sophisticated
level of behaviour, the more it does so by the suppression of
one pattern of linked emotions by another. Thus the pattern
of linked emotions associated with the dependent group can
be used to render difficult or impossible the obtrusion of the
patterns of emotion linked as they are in the fight-flight and
pairing groups.

THE WORK GROUP

In some groups that I have taken, what I have been calling
the 'sophisticated group' has been spontaneously called the
'work group'. The name is short, and expresses well an important aspect of the phenomena I wish to describe, so that
in future I shall use it instead of 'sophisticated group'. When
a group meets, it meets for a specific task, and in most human
activities today co-operation has to be achieved by sophisticated means. As I have already pointed out, rules of procedure are adopted; there is usually an established administrative machinery operated by officials who are recognizable
as such by the rest of the group, and so on. The capacity for
co-operation on this level is great, as anybody's experience
of groups will show. But it is different in kind from the
capacity for co-operation which is evidence on the basic-
assumption level. In my experience the psychological structure of the work group is very powerful, and it is noteworthy
that it survives with a vitality that would suggest that fears
that the work group will be swamped by the emotional states
proper to the basic assumptions are quite out of proportion.

I said earlier that the group from the first struggled hard to maintain a sophisticated structure, and that the effort put into this indicated the strength of the emotions associated with the basic assumptions. I still think this is so, but also believe that fears for the structure of the work group are expressions of ignorance of the forces with which the work group has to contend. The therapeutic group should have its attention constantly drawn to the fear of the basic-assumption group, and be shown that the object of the fear depends a great deal on the state of mind that is uppermost in the groups. Thus, if the dependent group is most in evidence—indeed, in evidence to the point at which the group appears to be identified with the dependent group—then fear is of the work group. Just as the emotions in the basic-assumption group appear to be linked together, so the mental phenomena of the work group appear to be linked together. Certain ideas play a prominent part in the work group: not only is the idea of 'development' rather than 'full equipment by instinct' an integral part of it, but so is the idea of the value of a rational or scientific approach to a problem. So also, as an inevitable concomitant of the idea of 'development', is accepted the validity of learning by experience. If, however, the group is identified with the dependent basic assumption, then all these ideas are feared, not of course simply as ideas but as activities at work within the group The dependent group soon shows that an integral part of its structure is a belief in the omniscience and omnipotence of some one member of the group. Any investigation of the nature of this belief arouses reactions which are reminiscent, to put it no higher, of the controversies of religion versus science. Indeed, investigation of this point is, as I suggested earlier, a scientific investigation of the religion of the group. Activities of the work group that would seem to involve investigation of the nature of the group deity—usually the psychiatrist—are met with a great variety of response, but, if one takes the response as a whole, one might imagine that Gibbon's description of the homoousian controversy was really a report on a therapeutic group session with the dependent basic assumption in action. Perhaps it was. Indeed, it may be helpful for any psychiatrist who has a taste for trying my methods in a group to remember that few things in history have aroused a group's feelings more powerfully than controversy about the characteristics of the deity whose cult is at the time flourishing. I should perhaps add that by flourishing I mean negatively as well as positively, that is, when the group is atheistic as well as when it is theistic. It is essential that the psychiatrist should be firm in drawing attention to the reality of the group's claims upon him, no matter how fantastic their elucidation makes those claims appear to be, and then to the reality of the hostility which is aroused by his elucidation. It is on occasions such as this that one can see both the strength of the emotions associated with the basic assumption and the vigour and vitality which can be mobilized by the work group. It is almost as if human beings were aware of the painful and often fatal consequences of having to act without an adequate grasp of reality, and therefore were aware of the need for truth as a criterion in the evaluation of their findings.

We must now consider some aspects of the part played by the work group in combination with one basic assumption in suppressing the overt activity of the other two basic assumptions. What is the fate of the two basic assumptions that are not operative? I propose to link this question with the question I left unanswered earlier about the nature and origin of the combination in which emotions were held in their association with any basic assumption. I said then that there were no observations at present available to the psychiatrist to explain why emotions associated with a basic assumption were held in combination with each other with such tenacity and exclusiveness. In order to explain this linkage and at the same time to explain the fate of the inoperative basic assumptions, I propose to postulate the existence of 'proto-mental' phenomena. I cannot represent my view adequately without proposing a concept that transcends experience. Clinically, I make a psychological approach, and therefore note phenomena only when they present themselves as psychological manifestations. Nevertheless, it is convenient to me to consider that the emotional state precedes the basic assumption and follows certain proto-mental phenomena of which it is an expression. Even this statement is objectionable because it establishes a more rigid order of cause and effect than I wish to subscribe to, for clinically it is useful to consider these events as links in a circular series; sometimes it is convenient to think that the basic assumption has been activated by consciously expressed thoughts, at others in strongly stirred emotions, the outcome of proto-mental activity. There is no harm in commencing the series where we choose if it throws light on what takes place. Starting, then, at the level of proto-mental events we may say that the group develops until its emotions become expressible in psychological terms. It is at this point that I say the group behaves 'as if' it were acting on a basic assumption.

In the proto-mental system there exist prototypes of the three basic assumptions, each of which exists as a function of the individual's membership of the group, each existing as a whole in which no part can be separated from the rest. Only at a different level, at a level where the events emerge as psychological phenomena, does there appear to be possible a differentiation of the components of each basic assumption, and on this level we can talk about feelings of fear or security or depression or sex, or other such.

The proto-mental system I visualize as one in which physical and psychological or mental are undifferentiated. It is a matrix from which spring the phenomena which at first appear—on a psychological level and in the light of psychological investigation—to be discrete feelings only loosely associated with one another. It is from this matrix that emotions proper to the basic assumption flow to reinforce, pervade, and, on occasion, to dominate the mental life of the group. Since it is a level in which physical and mental are undifferentiated, it stands to reason that, when distress from this source manifests itself, it can manifest itself just as well in physical forms as in psychological. The inoperative basic assumptions are confined within the proto-mental system; that is to say that if the sophisticated group is suffused with the emotions associated with the dependent basic assumption then the flight-fight and pair basic assumptions are confined within the limitations of the proto-mental phase. They are the victims of a conspiracy between the sophisticated group and the operating basic assumption. It is only the proto-mental stage of the dependent group that has been free to develop into the differentiated state where the psychiatrist can discern its operation as a basic assumption.

It is these proto-mental levels that provide the matrix of group diseases. These diseases manifest themselves in the individual but they have characteristics that make it clear that it is the group rather than the individual that is stricken, in much the same way, only in the opposite sense, as in the flight-fight group it always appears that it is the group rather than the individual that is being preserved. Briefly, what all this amounts to is that in any given group the matrix for the dis-eases that are present must be sought in two places—one is in the individual's relationship with the basic-assumption group and with himself as a participant in the maintenance of that group: the other is in the proto-mental stages of the other two basic assumptions.

To make my meaning still clearer I shall take an analogy from physical medicine, which, if it is remembered that I use it only as an analogy, may serve to make my meaning clear. Let us assume the case of the patient who is suffering from anxiety symptoms. In the course of the examination it appears that in addition to various psychological difficulties the patient has a fine tremor of the hands; let us assume that further examination shows signs of a thyrotoxicosis sufficiently serious to make a physical approach the method of choice in deciding treatment. In ordinary parlance it would be said that the disease had a physical origin. I would prefer to say that the matrix of the disease lay in the sphere of proto-mental events and that if the patient were seen so early that by average present-day standards no signs of disease cognizable by techniques either of physical medicine or of psychiatry were present, then the patient was presenting a very good example, *in petto*, of what I mean by the stage of proto-mental events in which physical and psychological are as yet undifferentiated and from which, in certain circumstances, group diseases, with physical and psychological components, have their origin. Where my analogy breaks down in expressing my view is in presenting the sphere of proto-mental events as bounded by the individual; in my opinion the sphere of proto-mental events cannot be understood by reference to the individual alone, and the intelligible field of study for the dynamics of proto-mental events is the individuals met together in a group. The proto-mental stage in the individual is only a part of the proto-mental system, for proto-mental phenomena are a function of the group and must therefore be studied in the group.

In advancing the concept of a proto-mental system I set out to account for the solidity with which all the emotions

of one basic assumption seemed to be welded together, and
at the same time to provide a concept that would account
for the whereabouts of inoperative basic assumptions that
were obviously felt by a group to be potentially active,
and must therefore be considered to be 'somewhere'. But
I have often found it useful after a postulation of this
kind to see what happens if I try to use the new theory for
purposes for which it was *not*, in origination, intended. For
this purpose I find an indulgence in speculation as good a
test field as any other, and I hope by this that I may come
nearer to deciding whether to regard the idea of a proto-
mental system as only a theory to draw together my
observations, a hypothesis to stimulate further investigation,
or a clinically observable fact.

My first speculation must concern what constitutes an intelligible field of study. The small therapeutic group cannot
do so as long as my technique is no further developed than
it is at present, and even if it were developed further, or if I
were to improve my powers of observation, it would still
remain a matter of doubt whether it were not wiser to seek
a solution in some other field. Before Freud, the attempts to
advance the study of neurosis were largely sterile because
the individual was considered to be an intelligible field of
study, but it was when Freud began to seek a solution in the
relationship between two people, the study of the transference, that he found what was the intelligible field of study
for at least some of the problems that the neurotic patient
poses, and problems that had hitherto defied all attempts at
solution began to have a meaning. The investigation then
commenced has continued to spread in depth and width. The
small therapeutic group is an attempt to see whether any
further results could be yielded by changing the field of study.
It will be necessary at some time to consider the use that the
group itself makes of manipulations of the field of study, but

for the moment I wish to consider the possibilities of changing the field again in order to see if it is possible by doing so to get new light on the small therapeutic group. The small therapeutic group does not produce evidence about physical disease fast enough for my purpose and does not produce enough of it. I prefer, therefore, to base my speculations on what might be found in a group large enough for statistical evidence of disease to be available (see Toynbee, 1935, pp. 12, 17). I should like to have evidence about such diseases as tuberculosis, venereal diseases, diabetes, and others, particularly with regard to such aspects of fluctuations in numbers of cases, virulence, and distribution as were not readily explicable in terms of anatomy, physiology, and other disciplines that are normally the stock-in-trade of Public Health investigations. Furthermore it would be necessary to have statistics that were valid at the significant moment.

In what follows I propose to use the letters *ba* to indicate the basic assumption and its associated emotional state. The basic assumption of dependence will be indicated by the letters *baD*, of pairing by *baP*, and of flight-fight by *baF*. For the proto-mental system I propose to use the letters *pm;* thus *pmDP* would mean that I referred to a state in which the basic assumptions of dependence and pairing were no longer cognizable as psychiatric phenomena, but were confined in some sort of latent phase, at present unelucidated, in the proto-mental system where physical and mental are undifferentiated. Similarly with *pmPF*, or *pmDF*. For the sophisticated or work group I shall use *W*.

(*a*) Suppose that a disease *X* springs from the proto-mental stage of dependent and pairing groups when suppressed by basically expressed *baF*. In my theory the disease *X* will be affiliated with *D* and *P* groups and, therefore, when it becomes overt, will have psychological affiliations with the emotions of *baP* and *baD*. Further, it will have a matrix which in this instance will be *pmD* and *pmP*. It will also have a psychological cause which will lie in *baP*. This does not mean that I consider that all diseases have a psychological cause, which is equal in importance with other causes, but I do consider that for the sake of completeness a disease should be so classified that we know not only the facts ordinarily described in medicine but also (i) its matrix, that is to say, in the example that I have given, *pmD* and *pmP*, (ii) its psychological affiliations, in my imaginary case, *baD* and *baP*, and (iii) its psychological cause, in this example, *baF*.

Similarly, I would add that we need to know the affiliation of the physical disease with other physical diseases, other than the already well-known affiliations arrived at from a study of anatomy and physiology, and that we must seek these other affiliated physical diseases by considering what other physical diseases can be classified, in the example I have given, as:

Matrix	*pmD* and *pmP*
Affiliation	*baD* and *baP*
Cause	*baF*

This should give us the affiliations of one physical disease with another, which are functions, not of anatomy, physiology, and bacteriology—nor yet of psychopathology—but of the individual's membership of a group.

(*b*) Since my thesis depends on the argument that there is a stage in which physical and mental are undifferentiated, it follows that, when disease manifests itself physically, say, as tuberculosis, there is a psychological counterpart or reciprocal, the exact nature of which is yet to be investigated, but which we may in this discussion assume to be *baD*. This reciprocal cannot be either cause or effect, for, if it is either one or the other, it must derive from an entirely different series of proto-mental events, or else from the operative basic assumption. The mental events to which tuberculosis is affiliated are necessarily, in my definition, neither cause nor effect; they are derivatives and developments from the same proto-mental phenomena as those from which tuberculosis itself arises. Tuberculosis is known to be very sensitive to developments in the psychology of a group, numbers fluctuating in what appears to be some kind of sympathy with the changes in mentality of the group. The disease demands prolonged care and nursing and the diet has reminiscences of man's earliest gastronomic experiences. It should be and is associated with many of the characteristics of *baD*, individuals reacting to their disorder and the limitations it imposes on them very much in the way that individuals with a similar personality react to *baD*. The existence of these facts has led often, before a tubercular lesion was demonstrated, to suggestion that the patient was malingering (Wittkower, 1949), or to use my terminology, that *baD* is the teleological cause of the patient's disorder, but for reasons I have given I cannot regard *baD* as a cause of any kind; it is the mental state with which tuberculosis is affiliated, and is therefore neither cause nor effect. To find the cause of the complaint—I refer, of course, to the cause as it is to be understood as a part of the scheme I am elaborating, and not to the perfectly well-known and well-established causes with which medicine is familiar—it would be necessary to correlate the fluctuations in the incidence of the disease with the *ba* prevalent in the group at the various times at which the figures for the disease were obtained. Let us assume that the highest figures corresponded always with *baF*. We should then classify tuberculosis as having, besides the already established characteristics,

Cause	*baF*
Affiliation	*baD*
Matrix	*pmDP*

Any attempt to make this sort of classification would clearly depend on opinion at best, wild guesswork at worst; but I think the attempt will need to be made: the attempt to be scientific must be adjusted to the state of immaturity of the study and this applies particularly to evaluation of the *ba* at any given moment.

So far I have been arguing that the concept of a proto- mental system, together with the theories of basic assumptions, might be used to provide a fresh slant on physical disease and particularly those diseases which have been called psychosomatic or have been considered as a part of psycho-social medicine and sociodynamics (see Halliday, 1948, pp. 142 *et seq.*). But if we can widen the field of study of physical disease to include the study of basic assumptions, proto-mental system, and the rest, in order to arrive at a fuller understanding of physical disorder, we can equally well use the same widened field to carry out the process in reverse. For it must be remembered that, if, as far as psycho- logical disorder is concerned, the system is postulated as proto-mental, it is equally, from the point of view of physical disease, proto-physical. Nevertheless, it may be possible more easily to find a technique for investigating the proto-mental system as the matrix for physical disorder by an investiga- tion making a physical approach. If, by using a physical approach, we can investigate the physical aspect of the proto- mental system, we may find a way of sampling what the proto-mental system of a group contains at any given time, and from that make the further step that would consist in elaborating a technique for observing the proto-mental counterparts of mental events. Any developments of this nature would make it possible to estimate what the psychological state of a group would be likely to become, because we could investigate it long before it emerged as a basic assumption basically expressed. To me this is important, for one characteristic that differentiates the patient group from other groups is the tendency of the patient group to act on basic assumptions basically.

Thanks to the British National Health Service, patients are able to feel that they have effectually dealt with all problems that arise from the financial element in the relationships with each other and with the doctor. Even so, there are occasions when financial problems are mentioned, usually as if they were affairs of domestic concern to the individual but none the less susceptible of interpretation as material expressing indirectly some aspect of the mental life of the group and of the individual in it. I propose, therefore, to continue in the sphere of money my speculations on the proto-mental system by seeing if I can use this concept, in a manner parallel to that in which I have already employed it, in the sphere of physical disease.

It has been said that 'The medium of exchange may be almost anything provided that it is generally acceptable,' (Clay, 1916, p. 164). It is not only a medium of exchange but also the standard of value. Recent work on primitive money has shown that it did not arise as a development of barter, nor yet even as a part of trade. On the contrary, trade, in its search for a medium that was generally acceptable and had an established value, adopted for its use currency, which was primarily an invention to facilitate the transactions of *wergild* and bride-price. 'It would be extravagant to claim that "bride-price" and *wergild* brought currency into existence, but they certainly established standards of value and regularized certain media of exchange . . .' (Hingston Quiggin, 1949, pp. 7 *et seq.*). Einzig, discussing this matter, says that possibly objects were chosen for currency because they were generally desired as an article of consumption or ornament but adds that the high degree of acceptability may have been due to non-commercial considerations such as the fact that an object could be used for religious sacrifices, for political payments (fines, tribute, blood-money), or for bride-money (Einzig, pp. 353 *et seq.*).

Both *wergild* and bride-price can be regarded as compensations to a group for loss of one of its members, and, looked at in this light, they reflect the supremacy of the group over the individual as in *baF*. Equally, *wergild* may be regarded as an expression of the value the community sets upon the individual, so that it could be interpreted on some occasions as an aspect of *baF* and on others as an expression of *baD;* similarly, bride-price can be regarded as an expression of *baP*. I am not, however, concerned at the moment to ascribe either institution to a particular *ba*—that would be the task of clinical observation—but to suggest the possibility that, just as in the discussion of physical disease, there may be grounds for enlisting my theories as a means of adding knowledge and understanding of disease to the knowledge already obtainable through the discipline of physical medicine, so there may be grounds for using my theories to add knowledge of disease of mechanisms of exchange to the knowledge already obtainable through the discipline of economics. For if the source of value of money lies not only in intrinsic value, and other sources discussed by Einzig, of the objects used for money but also in the bas, then we should expect that the psychological value might be different in *baF* from its value in *baP* or *baD* and so on. Furthermore, we might expect that the value of any currency might fluctuate, through fluctuations in value at the source from which money derives its psychological value—the basic assumptions. If we could determine clinically the nature of the value of money in *baF*, *baD*, and *baP* we might be able to trace the source of one of the causes of fluctuations in value of money as used in trade.

Now, one of the advantages of studying money, in the big group, is that it may be susceptible of statistical approach; whether the statistics available are any less open to criticism, on the grounds of lack of sensitivity, than the statistics of disease is doubtful, but yet a start must be made, and by someone who has statistical training and ability. But the real value of establishing some kind of correlation between fluctuations in value of money and changes in *ba* would arise if it were found that there was some correlation between patterns in the statistics of disease and statistics showing fluctuations in the value of money in the group. Obviously, any attempt to isolate fluctuations in value due to changes in value at the psychological source of monetary value, namely, its source in *wergild* and bride purchase from other sources from which money derived its value may prove to be very ambitious unless, as I suspect, value of currency reposes to a far greater extent than has been imagined on psychological foundations, and in particular on the dominant basic assumption and the *pm*. If such correlations were proved to exist, then one might reasonably feel that some evidence was being provided for taking the basic assumptions to be clinical entities, and this in turn might lead to some clarification of ideas about the nature of the proto-mental system.

In discussing the linkage of emotion in a *ba* I suggested that it was necessary to regard any feeling, such as anxiety, as differing according to the *ba* of which it was a part: similarly we must consider that the value of money in, say, *baD* differs from the value of money in *baF*, and by this I mean that its value differs in respect of quality as well as quantity. What I mean by this may be seen if we consider the attitude to money and the value that is set on it in a religious group where W is sufficiently strong to call baD into full activity and compare this value with the value that is set on money in a nation at war when baF is in full activity. In the latter the value of money is linked with its convertibility into munitions of war, in the former with its value in offsetting feelings of guilt for dependence beyond reasonable time-limits, and on parents more than human by the purchase of feelings of virtue. In baP it would appear to lie in its ability to facilitate, by bride-purchase or dowry, the acquisition of a mate.

My speculations appear to suggest that the concepts of basic assumptions and proto-mental systems hold promise of facilitating inquiry in areas other than those from which they were derived, but, before acting on the assumption that a case for further investigation is established, it may be as well to check our speculations by bringing them into closer relationship with fact. The glaring difficulty is to state what basic assumption is operative in a large group; for example, are we to say that the ba in a nation at war is baF? And if so, is it true that this would hold for all parts of the nation—for example, the agricultural community? If we assume that a nation at war exemplifies baF, are we to assume that the nation in question provides an intelligible field of study for the phenomena associated with that basic assumption? Where shall we seek statistical evidence of fluctuations in disease? What statistical material will reveal fluctuations in the value of currency and where, in time, would we expect to find those fluctuations in the value of currency, or the incidence of disease, that we would expect to be correlated, if correlated they are, with the basic assumption of, say, August, 1939?

Though it may seem a far cry from a study of the small patient group, it may be worth while trying to relate these theories to the recent history of the large group, to see if they stand the test of practicable application to actual events, before attempting a more ambitious project involved in making them the subject of statistical research.

REFERENCES

CLAY, HENRY (1916). *Economics for the General Reader.* London: Macmillan.

A good short account of money from the standpoint of the economist.

EINZIG, PAUL (1949). *Primitive Money.* London: Eyre & Spottiswoode.

Einzig is more cautious than Hingston Quiggin, and, though he reaches substantially the same conclusion, he draws attention to the many sources on which money can depend for its value: it is a wholesome corrective to any facile generalization. I am inclined to think that the concept of the basic assumptions might throw light on a subject the complexity of which is better displayed by Einzig than by Hingston Quiggin.

GIBBON, EDWARD (1781). *The Decline and Fall of the Roman Empire.* London: Methuen, 1909 Edition. Vol. II. Page 373.

An historical study of disputes about the nature and attributes of deity would go far to clarify many of the points I would like to make about the nature of *baD*.

HALLIDAY, J. L. (1948). *Psychosocial Medicine.* New York: Norton; London: Heinemann, 1949.

HINGSTON QUIGGIN, A. (1949). *A Survey of Primitive Money.* London: Methuen.

HODGKIN, R. H. (1935). *History of Anglo-Saxons*. London: Oxford University Press. Vol. 2. Page 579.

PETIT-DUTAILLIS (1911). *Studies Supplementary to Stubbs' Constitutional History*. Manchester University Press. Pages 36-38.

Although the subject is a commonplace in most studies of constitutional history there is little material in any of it which is really helpful in providing either confirmation or refutation of any attempt to relate *Wergild* with a basic assumption.

TOYNBEE, ARNOLD (1935). *A Study of History*. Oxford, 1935 Edition. Vol. I.

Toynbee's discussion of what constitutes an intelligible field of study in history can be taken to apply equally well to the study of the psychology of the group.

WITTKOWER, ERIC (1949). *A Psychiatrist Looks at Tuberculosis*. London: The National Association for the Prevention of Tuberculosis.

This study provides plenty of material on which to form tentative judgments about the validity of my theories of the psychological affiliations of disease.

6

In this article I would discuss one or two points about the small therapeutic group; let us consider the vicissitudes of an interpretation. If a psycho-analyst were to conduct a group by my method he would soon be impressed by the apparent futility of it; it seems impossible to achieve precision by interpretation, for even when the formulation of the interpretation is satisfying there seems small reason to suppose it reaches its destination. At first, in an attempt to counteract what I thought was some sort of resistance which patients were achieving through use of the group, I used to be beguiled into giving individual interpretations as in psychoanalysis. In doing this I was doing what patients often do—trying to get to individual treatment. True, I was trying to get to it as a doctor, but in fact this can be stated in terms of an attempt to get rid of the 'badness' of the group and, for the doctor, the 'badness' of the group is its apparent unsuitability as a therapeutic instrument—which is, as we have already seen, the complaint also of the patient. Ignoring those inherent qualities of the group which appear to give substance to the complaint, and choosing instead to regard this unsuitability as a function of the failure of the doctor or patient to use the group in a therapeutic way, we can see that the failure, at the moment when the analyst gives in to his impulse to make individual interpretations, lies in being

influenced by *baD* instead of interpreting it, for, as soon as I
start to give supposedly psycho-analytic interpretations to
an individual, I reinforce the assumption that the group consists of patients dependent on the doctor, which is the *baD*.

We can now see what it is that gives rise to the feeling of
imprecision when making interpretations; it is the realization
that the group is influenced by that aspect of the doctor's
contribution which falls in with the basic assumption and
hardly at all by the part of it that consists of interpretation
of the behaviour of the group. In trying to achieve precision
of aim I was really suffering, as all members of the group
suffer, through dislike of the emotional quality in myself and
in the group that is inherent in membership of the human
group. This quality is a kind of capacity for co-operation
with the group, but I propose from now on to reserve the
word 'co-operation' for conscious or unconscious working
with the rest of the group in work, whereas for the capacity
for spontaneous instinctive co-operation in the basic assumptions, one example of which is what we have just been discussing. I shall use the word 'valency'.

VALENCY

I mean to indicate, by its use, the individual's readiness to
enter into combination with the group in making and acting
on the basic assumptions; if his capacity for combination is
great, I shall speak of a high valency, if small, of a low
valency; he can have, in my view, *no* valency only by ceasing
to be, as far as mental function is concerned, human.
Although I use this word to describe phenomena that are
visible as, or deducible from, psychological events, yet I wish
also to use it to indicate a readiness to combine on levels that
can hardly be called mental at all but are characterized by
behaviour in the human being that is more analogous to

tropism in plants than to purposive behaviour such as is implicit in a word like 'assumption'. In short, I wish to use it for events in the *pm* system should need arise.

When I gave in to the impulse to give individual interpretations, my leadership of the group was more an expression of distress than an illumination of external reality clearly perceived. My contribution to *W* was diminished, to *baD* increased, and thus the 'patient' component in my contribution as a whole had been increased.

I deal with this situation by assuming that everyone in the group is suffering in the same way and, giving up making supposedly psycho-analytic interpretations, I interpret only that aspect of the individual's contribution which shows that the individual, in attempting, say, to get help for his problem, is leading the group to establish the *baD* or, alternatively, to shift to *baP* or *baF*.

By doing this I have both decreased the 'patient' component in my leadership and drawn the attention of the individuals concerned to the dilemma that results from membership of the group. Consequences flow from both these facts, but for the time being I ignore both in the actual group situation, and, in this description, the consequences that follow on the decrease of the 'patient' component in my behaviour.

THE DILEMMA OF THE INDIVIDUAL

By concentrating on that aspect of the individual's contribution which is a function of his valency, I reduce the group—with a speed that varies in direct proportion to the degree of sophistication that the group has achieved in this kind of therapy—to taking refuge in puerilities and finally in silence.

I shall not spend time describing commonplaces of interpretation, such as those necessary for illustrating feelings of

guilt that arise from the idea that interpretations of behaviour are really expressions of disapproval; the point that
must be demonstrated is that individuals experiencing this
dilemma are intimidated by it and are thus displaying their
fear of the basic assumptions and the part they themselves
play in their maintenance; this fear is intimately linked with
the sense of inadequacy to group life that accompanies increased insight into the hitherto unsuspected complexities
of participation in the human group. I demonstrate this
dilemma of the individual—with intermissions during the
various periods when other group phenomena are presenting
with more urgency—throughout the entire course of the
group's existence. Although no change takes place in the
situation, individuals do gradually become less oppressed by
the sense of being impaled on one or other horn of the
dilemma and less obstructed in active participation in the
group. One interesting result of increasing familiarity of the
dilemma of the individual is the demonstration that there is
no way in which the individual can, in a group, 'do nothing'
—not even by doing nothing. So we have come round once
more, though from a different angle, to our suspicion that
all members of a group are responsible for the behaviour of
the group (see p. 58).

In practice matters do not develop so smoothly as my
description suggests, for, as I indicated, for weeks and months
at a time other aspects of the group obtrude and demand
attention, if for no other reason, for the reason that they are
obtruding and therefore best lend themselves to demonstration. Amongst these other phenomena is the consequence
that flows from the diminished 'patient' component in the
therapist's contribution, and to this I must now turn.

It will be remembered that groups claim from time to time
that I am the patient and suggest sometimes that I have
benefited by the group experience. One element that con-

tributes to this expression of their belief is envy that I am apparently better able to turn my experience of the group to good account than others are and become by virtue of this approximated to Aristotle's 'political animal', thereby achieving the growth and development that are the concomitant of being an organism in its proper environment; perhaps I typify the patient who is obtaining more than his fair share of care and it is some such belief that makes the group pick on another member as leader. Be that as it may, the new leader is, in my experience without exception, a thoroughgoing psychiatric case. He is extolled for keeping the group going; for talking freely; for being, in short, a great improvement on myself in a variety of ways. Though there is always substance in these appreciative comments, there has never been any question that the man or woman thrown up by the group is a 'case'.

We have reached this position: the group is engaged in sustaining, placating, soothing, flattering, and deferring to its most ill member, who is now the leader; we must regard this development as the dual of *baD*, and to a further consideration we must accordingly turn.

THE DUAL OF *baD*

The simple aspect of *baD* is presented when all the individuals in the group look to myself as a person with whom each has an exclusive relationship. There is little overt contact between the individuals, and all facts that conflict with the idea that I solve all the individual's problems and have a particular concern for the individual's welfare are denied, not simply verbally but by a kind of mass inertia that precludes stimulation by facts that are not appropriate to the emotions of *baD*. Among such undesired facts are interpretations, whether given by myself or another, that carry the implication that my assumed pre-eminence in experience of groups is itself a matter for scrutiny. When the group can no longer ignore these interpretations, it sometimes sweeps them into the *baD* system by treating me as a baby that has to be humoured by indulgence in its self-display. This brings into play the state that I have described as the dual of the 'simple' form of *baD*—I do not nourish and sustain the group so they nourish and sustain me. At this point I must explain a difficulty I have in giving the reader an idea of the evidence on which I base my hypothesis. Apart from the need to disguise actual incidents sufficiently to preserve anonymity for the individuals, I am bound so to describe an incident that it bears out my theory. I obviously must produce my hypothesis because I see events in a particular way, and there is no proof that the way I see them is accurate. The description then becomes little more than a repetition of a hypothesis clothed in terms of concrete events. I would find some means by which I could offer the reader something more convincing, and it is to this end that I propose, with what success I do not know, to find descriptions by other hands of situations which appear to me to be illustrations of phenomena that my hypotheses purport to illumine. I shall try to take examples from any time and any place; my first is from Toynbee's *A Study of History* (1948, Vol. I, pp. 141-144). By reference to this passage the reader can form his own opinion and compare it with events that I propound in the light of my theory. Briefly, Toynbee shows how Egypt was exhausted by the building of the pyramids under Kephron and his successors. Applying my theory, this situation would be described as a group movement to allay the anxiety state of the leader of the group. The nature of that anxiety is not immediately relevant but appears to be centred on the death of the leader and the need to deny its reality.

For my immediate purpose the interesting thing is the sub-sequent development in the group, namely the extension of the treatment received by the Pharaoh to ever-increasing numbers of members of the group so that, as Toynbee says, quite ordinary people receive the same treatment as the Pharaohs—just as good, but at a much cheaper rate. A change in the technique thus brought all the benefits of the very exclusive psychotherapy of the Pharaohs within the reach of quite moderate purses. It looks as if those of us who seek to find in group therapy a solution of the economic problems posed by psycho-analysis are really following a tradition of very respectable age. This situation, in which a whole people is exhausted to provide for one individual, is what I would describe as the dual of *baD*. We may see in it the extent to which coping with the *baD* absorbs energies of the group which might have been devoted to the external realities of group security had no technique been available for a more direct management of the *baD*.

We shall have to examine these matters more closely when we come to consider *W* and particularly some specialized forms of work group, but for the present I must leave these aside to consider the complication that has been introduced by the close connection in *baD* between the leadership of the group and the most psychiatrically dis-ordered member of the group. I do not wish to attempt any solution of the problem of why the group, when left to spontaneous behaviour, chooses as its leader, in *baD*, its most ill member. It has always been well recognized that this is so; so much so in fact that the great religious leader—and the religious group for obvious reasons is a group in which *baD* is active and vital—is commonly assumed to be mad or possessed of a devil, exactly as if members of a group with *baD* in the ascendant felt that if they were not led by a mad-man, then they ought to be. Indeed one could say that, just as they reject all facts that run counter to the belief that they are all individually looked after by the person or deity on whom they depend, so they reject all facts that might indicate that the leader or deity was sane. The belief in the holiness of idiots, the belief that genius is akin to madness, all indicate this same tendency of the group to choose, when left unstructured, its most ill member as its leader. Perhaps it is an unconscious recognition that the baby, if only we had not become accustomed to associating its behaviour with its physical development, is really insane, and in the *baD* it is as necessary to have someone who is dependent as it is to have someone on whom to depend.

ANXIETY OF THE WORK GROUP

The immediate point, to which I shall return later when I come to deal in detail with *W*, is that the group that has most experience of dealing with *baD*, namely the religious group or priesthood, always deals with this problem of the leader in *baD* as if it were handling dynamite. The attempt is constantly and increasingly made to ensure that the leader in *baD* is not a concrete person—the commonest way in which this is done is of course by making a god the leader; and when that, for a variety of reasons, turns out still to be not sufficiently immaterial, by striving to make him God, a spirit. The essence of the attempt, in my opinion, is to prevent the group from doing either one of two things: (i) making a choice of an actual man; (ii) allowing the choice to be made by 'unconstitutional' means, that is to say, by a spontaneous act of choice in which the emotions are not cooled by the discipline involved in, for example, election by ballot. The priesthood, which, as I say, is the *W* group most experienced in dealing with the *baD*, strives, with very rare exceptions, to avoid both these points while making some concession to the group demand for an actual concrete person. Even the exceptions suggest that the priesthood is well aware, if unconsciously, of the danger; the prophet Samuel disapproved of the clamour to end the Israelitish theocracy and, when he had to give in, ensured that the leader would be chosen by methods that violate both canons. It was a subtle and successful revenge, and the results were all that could be desired by way of picking a psychiatric winner.

THE CAUSE OF ANXIETY

But against what danger is the priesthood striving to protect the group? It is not, I submit, merely the danger inherent in incompetent leadership; for one thing, leadership by the mentally disordered is by no means always incompetent— far from it. But apart from that I hope to show that there are far more weighty reasons why the priesthood should fear the spontaneous development of leadership in baD. To demonstrate this I must return again to experiences in the small therapeutic group.

In its search for a leader the group finds a paranoid schizophrenic or malignant hysteric if possible; failing either of these, a psychopathic personality with delinquent trends will do; failing a psychopathic personality it will pick on the verbally facile high-grade defective. I have at no time experienced a group of more than five people that could not provide a good specimen of one of these.

Once the leader is discovered the group treats him or her with some deference, and the occasional spicing of flattery —'Mr. So-and-so always keeps the discussion going so well' —serves to reinforce his position as leader. There is usually some tendency to test me for signs of jealousy, but this phase quickly passes. A comment that is often heard is that the group 'could not do without' Miss X or Mr. Y, as the case might be. This comment is also made about myself. Though it appears to be insignificant enough, it is a matter to which we shall have to pay considerable attention later.

When the leadership of the individual concerned is well established in the eyes of all members of the group, difficulties arise. King Saul, the frogs, in Aesop, who would have a stork for king, the Pharaohs, all in varying degrees illustrate aspects of the group in its new situation. As I showed before, the group turns to myself. It is of course not only the priesthood that is alarmed at this situation. Whenever a state exists that is likely to activate, or itself to have been activated by, the *baD*, there is a fear of dictatorship—a recent example is the often expressed fear that the Welfare State will lead to a tyrannical interference with liberty—the seizure of power by Communists, bureaucrats, etc. One of the most common calls in this situation is for a return to a belief in God, and indeed it will be surprising if in the small therapeutic group some member does not make this very plea. It expresses the desire to avoid the concrete embodiment of leadership in an actual member of the group. If I leave things to develop, many remedies will be proposed; revolt against the chosen leader, a claim that treatment should be available for all and that one person should not monopolize, and so on. In effect practically all the solutions adumbrated are recognizable as closely similar to procedures tried throughout history. What is not so easy to describe is what it is against which the group is seeking to protect itself.

EMOTIONAL OSCILLATION IN A GROUP

My conclusion is that the situation derives from the stimulus produced by having, on the *W* level of the therapeutic group, leader and psychiatrist in one. The group is compelled to recognize that the spontaneously chosen leader is seriously disordered—as I mentioned earlier, it seems to be essential that in *baD* the leader should be 'mad'; or—a description the group finds more flattering to itself and the individual concerned—a 'genius'. At the same time it is compelled to believe that he is the dependable leader. Now, this can only be done by a series of oscillations from one view to the other. If I refuse to intervene, and I have tested this situation several times by letting it go very far, even too far for safety, the oscillations become very rapid. And when, as in this situation, the distance separating the two beliefs is great— for it is hard to imagine two views more widely separated than a belief that the leader is mad and the belief that he is the dependable person on whom you rely for your welfare —then the oscillations have to be both rapid in time and large in excursion. The result is that the group can no longer contain the emotional situation, which thereupon spreads with explosive violence to other groups until enough groups have been drawn in to absorb the reaction. In practice in the small group this means impulsion to complain to outside authority, e.g. write to the press, or to a Member of Parliament, or to the authorities of the Clinic. The object of this drawing in of other groups is not, as I at first supposed it to be, revenge on the psychiatrist for discomfort—though that may be there, and damage to the psychiatrist or group may be the result—but to bring in so much inert material in the way of outsiders from the group, who do not share the emotional situation, that the new and much larger group ceases to vibrate. There is no longer the violent and disagreeable mass oscillation.

Obviously much depends on the speed with which the other groups or single groups, or even part of another group, can be brought in to absorb the oscillations. If they come in too slowly or in too small amounts, then the oscillations spread to the hitherto inert and the situation is more disagreeable than ever.

Clearly it is not desirable that such an explosion should take place and, in fact, except for reasons of research, it is not justifiable to let a reaction reach a point at which the group cannot contain its emotions. What is necessary is that the psychiatrist should find interpretations that give the group insight into what is going on; to bring the *ba* and *W* into contact.

Interpretations which expose, in detail and in the course of their development, the phenomena that I have here described in general terms seem to me to do this. The reader may find it entertaining to see if he can detect any situations that correspond to the description I have given of the *baD* and its dual in the reports of group activities, such as that which I have just used, not only in historical works but in contemporary reports such as newspaper accounts. In this country at any rate press comments on the Welfare State, so-called, seem to me often to betray an anxiety that the *baD* in either simple or dual form is being stimulated or is alternatively the source from which desires for a Welfare State spring. I should add, however, that it is much easier to believe one can see these phenomena in groups from which one is detached than in a small group in which one is actively participating. It is this latter experience which is the important one.

REFERENCES

TOYNBEE, ARNOLD (1934). *A Study of History* (2nd ed. 1948). Vol. I. London: Oxford University Press.

7

In the preceding section I described one cause of oscillation in a group. I wish now to consider a phenomenon that may lead either to such oscillation or else to schism. In my fifth article I said that 'development' was an important function of the W group. It is also one of the respects in which the W group differs from the basic-assumption group. The W group is necessarily concerned with reality and, therefore, might be said to have some of the characteristics Freud attributes to the ego in his discussion of the individual. Since the W group is concerned with reality, its techniques tend ultimately to be scientific. The point now is the resistance that is set up when development is demanded of the group or of the individuals composing it.

SCHISM

According to his personality, the individual adheres to one of two sub-groups. One sub-group opposes further advance, and in doing so appeals to loyalty to the dependent leader, or to the group bible, which, as we have seen, is a substitute for the dependent leader. The adherents of this sub-group appeal to tradition, 'the word of (the group) god', or to somebody who has been made into the group god in order to resist change. Members of this sub-group manipulate the dependent leader or substitutes they claim to support in such a way that adherence to the group will not demand any painful sacrifices and will therefore be popular. Mental activity thus becomes stabilized on a level that is platitudinous, dogmatic, and painless. Development is arrested and the resultant stagnation is widespread.

The reciprocal sub-group is composed of those ostensibly supporting the new idea and this sub-group sets out to achieve the same end as the first sub-group, but in a rather different manner; it becomes so exacting in its demands that it ceases to recruit itself. In this way there is none of the painful bringing together of initiated and uninitiated, primitive and sophisticated, that is the essence of the developmental conflict. Both sub-groups thus achieve the same end; the conflict is brought to an end. To exaggerate for the sake of clarity, I would say that the one sub-group has large numbers of primitive unsophisticated individuals who constantly add to their number, but who do not develop; the other sub-group develops, but on such a narrow front and with such few recruits that it also avoids the painful bringing together of the new idea and the primitive state. The mechanism equalizes the degree of sophistication in individuals in the community and also prevents the conflict between development and instinct in the individual. I am reminded of allegations that a society breeds copiously from its less cultured or less educated members, while the 'best' people remain obstinately sterile.

Schism, as I have described it in an extreme form here, should be contrasted with what takes place when the group tries to end oscillation by absorption of external groups (Section 6): the schismatic group attempts to solve its problem by internal war, the other by external war.

SOME OTHER VIEWS OF GROUPS

It may help if I now bring together the main themes of the foregoing and make a comparison with some of the many other views that have been put forward about groups.

The problem of the individual's relationship with others and with his group has been discussed from very early times. Plato emphasized the individual function in the group, that is to say, the need for the shoemaker to stick to his last for the harmonious life of the group. This view seems naïve when set by the side of the complexities of present-day psychology; but it can be forgotten that there is substance in this statement. It presupposes that individuals are rational people and that the governing consideration is the limitation imposed by reality. If the individual sticks to his task, if he co-operates with other individuals in letting them fulfil their tasks, then all will be well. In my terminology this would be the equivalent of saying that if the W group were the only component in the mental life of the group, then there would be no difficulty. But the point that I have made throughout these articles is that the W group is constantly perturbed by influences which come from other group mental phenomena.

That this was so became obvious at an early date, and the Platonic theory was felt to be unsatisfactory because it did not stand up to the test of experience. Notably it was criticized by Aristotle. But for our purposes I do not think that we need to consider any developments until St. Augustine produced *The City of God*. It is significant that the capture of Rome by Alaric should have produced so intense a reaction, and that the effect upon St. Augustine was to make him reconsider the whole question of human relationships within the state. What he does is to postulate a heavenly city in which the relationships between individuals become harmonized through each individual's relationship with God. Now this view is very different from that of Plato. St. Augustine has introduced a new dimension. His postulates imply that the Platonic description of what I call the W group is not a sufficient view of the group; what is needed is something very close to what I mean by the *baD*. I have already described how in *baD* individuals do not have a relationship with each other but each has it with the dependent leader. Since St. Augustine there has never been any real return to the classical view, although in some respects Hobbes comes near to ignoring the class of phenomena with which St. Augustine attempted to deal. Liberal thinkers of recent times have been disposed to argue that emotion and reason are easily harmonized, that is to say, in my terminology, that the operations of the W group can easily be harmonized with the operations of the basic-assumption group. Nietzsche appears to react against this view, seeming to suggest that a group achieves vitality only by the release of aggressive impulses. In my terminology this would mean a feeling of vitality could only be achieved by the dominance of the basic assumption, notably the *baF*. In my experience of groups all these views appear in one form or another to be expressed and even to gain a temporary ascendancy in action. But from what I have already said in these articles, it will be realized that I do not consider that any of them in practice provides any lasting solution. In any event, as I hope to be able to show, the group reactions are infinitely more complex than the foregoing theories, even in their full deployment, suggest. Freud expressly disavowed any but a superficial study of the group problem (*Group Psychology and the Analysis of the Ego*), basing his observations largely on a criticism, derived from psycho-analysis, of the work done by others (*Totem and Taboo*, 1950, p. 75, fn. 1).

In his *Group Psychology and the Analysis of the Ego*, Freud opens his discussion by pointing out that individual and group psychology cannot be absolutely differentiated because the psychology of the individual is itself a function of the individual's relationship to another person or object. He objects (p. 3) that it is difficult to attribute to the factor of number a significance so great as to make it capable by itself of moving in over mental life a new instinct that is otherwise not brought into play. In my view no new instinct is brought into play—it is always in play. The only point about collecting a group of people is that it enables us to see just how the 'political' characteristics of the human body operate. I have already said I do not consider it necessary for a number of people to be brought together—the individual cannot help being a member of a group even if his membership of it consists in behaving in such a way as to give reality to the idea that he does not belong to a group at all. In this respect the psycho-analytical situation is not 'individual psychology' but 'pair'. The individual is a group animal at war, not simply with the group, but with himself for being a group animal and with those aspects of his personality that constitute his 'groupishness'.

It is necessary for a group to meet in a room because the conditions for study can be provided only in that way. Freud and others whom he quotes, such as McDougall and Le Bon, seem to me to consider that group psychology is something which comes into being when there are a number of people collected together in the same place and at the same time, and in this respect I agree with Freud's protest that too much significance is thereby attributed to number; I think he is mistaken in saying that a solution must only be sought in one or other of the two alternatives:

(i) the possibility that the social instinct is not primitive, or

(ii) that its development begins in a manner such as that
of the family.

There is a third. I would say that the importance of the actual
group is similar to the importance of analyst and analysed:
it is necessary for an analysand to come to a psycho-analyst
in order that the transference relationship should be rendered
demonstrable. In the same way it is important that the group
should come together so that the characteristics of the group
and the individual in it should be demonstrable. I attach no
intrinsic importance to the coming together of the group. It
is important that the group should come together sufficiently
closely for me to be able to give an interpretation without
having to shout it. This means that the number must be
limited. The degree of dispersion of the group must similarly
be limited because I wish all individuals to have an opportunity of witnessing the evidence on which I base my interpretation. For the same reason the individuals must all collect
at the same time. Now this congregation of the group in a
particular place at a particular time is obviously very important for the purely mechanical reasons I have just given,
but it has no significance whatsoever in the production of
group phenomena. The idea that it has springs from the
erroneous impression that a thing must necessarily commence
at the moment when its existence becomes demonstrable.
The point that I would make is that no individual, however
isolated in time and space, can be regarded as outside a
group or lacking in active manifestations of group psychology, although conditions do not exist which would make
it possible to demonstrate it. Acceptance of the idea that the
human being is a group animal would solve the difficulties
that are felt to exist in the seeming paradox that a group is
more than the sum of its members. The explanation of
certain phenomena must be sought in the matrix of the
group and not in the individuals that go to make up the

group. Time-keeping is no function of any part, in isolation, of the mechanism of a clock, yet time-keeping is a function of the clock and of the various parts of the clock when held in combination with each other.

There is no more need to be confused by the impression that a group is more than the sum of its members than it would be to be confused by the idea that a clock is more than a collection of the parts that are necessary to make a clock.

To sum up, there are characteristics in the individual whose real significance cannot be understood unless it is realized that they are part of his equipment as a herd animal and their operation cannot be seen unless it is looked for in the intelligible field of study—which in this instance is the group. You cannot understand a recluse living in isolation unless you inform yourself about the group of which he is a member. To argue that in such a case one is not dealing with a group is merely to prove oneself naïvely imperceptive. For this reason I dislike the nomenclature used by Rickman of two-body, three-body, relationships. I think that such terms are liable to too naïve interpretation. The recluse is not, in my view, made more comprehensible by being viewed as part of a two-body situation, simply because he and the observer appear to be geographically alone together. I would want to know whether the recluse and observer were members of the same group and if not of what groups the two were members. Nor would I be in the least bit impressed by the fact that no other 'bodies' were visible. It may make my position still clearer if I say that this argument contributes to my objections to the psycho-analytic study of historical characters. The effects of any errors that may exist in psycho-analysis through disregard of group phenomena are likely to be moderated by the fact that analyst and analysand have many group tensions in common. An analyst today, even if he is aware of the importance of the knowledge of the circumstances of the person he is studying, cannot possibly have the feel of the situation in which an historical character lived and moved in the way the analyst can have a feeling for the situation in which his patient lives.

It appears to me that Freud is in some ways failing to realize, in his discussion of groups, the nature of the revolution he himself produced when he looked for an explanation of neurotic symptoms, not in the individual, but in the individual's relationship with objects. The whole point about looking at a group is that it changes the field of study to include phenomena that cannot be studied outside the group. Outside the group as a field of study, their activity is not manifest. The group, in the sense of a collection of people in a room, adds nothing to the individual or the aggregate of individuals—it merely reveals something that is not otherwise visible.

In other words the apparent difference between group psychology and individual psychology is an illusion produced by the fact that the group provides an intelligible field of study for certain aspects of individual psychology, and in so doing brings into prominence phenomena that appear alien to an observer unaccustomed to using the group. Freud does not appear to me to state anywhere that his views of the group are derived from a study of animism; he states that his contribution is visible only in his selection both of material and opinions (presumably from the standard works he cites, *Totem and Taboo*, p. 75, note 1). Explanations of group behaviour appear to be derived by deductions from the psycho-analytic situation. It is possibly for this reason that Freud's description of the group, and still more that of Le Bon, whom Freud quotes with some approval, read somewhat strangely to me when I compare them with my actual experiences in a group. For example, when Freud quotes Le

Bon as saying 'Groups have never thirsted after truth. They demand illusions and cannot do without them' (Freud, 1921), I do not feel able to agree with that description. As I have pointed out at the commencement of this section, I attribute great force and influence to the work group, which through its concern with reality is compelled to employ the methods of science in no matter how rudimentary a form. I think one of the striking things about a group is that, despite the influence of the basic assumptions, it is the W group that triumphs in the long run. Freud himself appears to consider—notably when he discusses the part that the group plays in the production of language, folk song, folklore, etc.—that Le Bon's description is unfair to the group. When Freud criticizes McDougall's views on the highly organized group, he points out that McDougall considers that the conditions of organization remove 'the psychological disadvantages of group formation'. This comes very near to my view of the specialized work group as having as its function the manipulation of the basic assumption to prevent its obstruction of the work group. Freud prefers to describe the problem as consisting in procuring for the group 'precisely those features which were characteristic of the individual and which are extinguished in him by the formation of the group'. He postulates an individual outside the primitive group, who possessed his own continuity, his self-consciousness, his traditions and customs, his own particular functions and position. He says that owing to his entry into an 'unorganized' group, the individual had lost his distinctiveness for a time. In my view the struggle of the individual to preserve his distinctiveness assumes different characteristics according to the state of mind of the group at any given moment. Group organization should give stability and permanence to the work group, which is felt to be much more easily submerged by the basic assumptions if the group is unorganized. Individual distinctiveness is no part of life in a group acting on the basic assumptions. Organization and structure are weapons of the *W* group. They are the product of co-operation between members of the group, and their effect once established in the group is to demand still further co-operation from the individuals in the group. In this respect McDougall's organized group is always a work group and never a basic-assumption group. A group acting on a basic assumption needs no organization or co-operation. The counterpart of co-operation in the basic-assumption group is what I have called valency—a spontaneous, unconscious function of the gregarious quality in the personality of man. It is only when a group begins to act on a basic assumption that difficulties arise. Action inevitably means contact with reality, and contact with reality compels regard for truth and therefore imposes scientific method, and hence the evocation of the work group.

We may return to consider further the specialized work group. As I have suggested, Freud was handicapped by having to deduce group situations from his study of the transference. For reasons I have given, the transference is likely to be coloured by group characteristics deriving from *baP*; that is to say, if we consider group phenomena that are likely to be activated by the stimulus of the pair situation actually existing in psycho-analysis. Indeed, it is in tl e group situation that we can most easily find the source both of the prominence of sexual elements in psycho-analysis and of the suspicions and accusations of the opponents of Freud that psycho-analysis was 'sexual'. The immediate consequences for his discussion of groups is that he was able to deduce from psycho-analysis some of the characteristics of two specialized work groups, Army and Church, but was not led on to a discussion of the specialized work group most likely to have to deal with *baP*. The sub-group in a society that is most likely to have to deal with manifestations of *baP* is the sub-group which attaches most importance to breeding, namely the aristocracy. If work-group characteristics were to play a dominant role, they would be manifested by some activity such as subsidy of genetics research. As it is, we cannot regard the interest shown in breeding as having the scientific aura which should be pathognomic of the work group. The reason, of course, is that it is not dealing simply with the work-group problem. It is a specialized sub-group split off to deal with the *baP* in much the same way as the Army and the Church have to deal with *baF* and *BaD* respectively. For this reason, the relationship of this sub-group with the main group is not likely to be determined by the scientific accuracy with which it conducts its love affairs on strictly genetic principles, but rather on the efficiency with which it satisfies the group demand that the *baP* should be so dealt with that it does not obstruct the *W* functions of the group as a whole.

Now I have already said that in *baP* anxiety derives from the feeling that both group and individual are subservient to the unborn genius. The function of the aristocracy is sometimes to find an outlet for activity based on the assumption of the pairing group without outraging the reality sense of the group; sometimes to prevent the reality sense of the group from undermining the institutions on the preservation of which the group depends for provision of a harmless vehicle for an expression of *baP*.

REFERENCES

FREUD, S. (1913). *Totem and Taboo*. Trans. by J. Strachey. London: Hogarth, 1950.

FREUD, S. (1921). *Group Psychology and the Analysis of the Ego*. London: Hogarth, 1922. *Complete Works*, Vol. 18.

Re-View

Group Dynamics

Using his psycho-analytic experience Freud[1] attempted to illuminate some of the obscurities revealed by Le Bon, Mc-Dougall, and others in their studies of the human group. I propose to discuss the bearing of modern developments of psycho-analysis, in particular those associated with the work of Melanie Klein, on the same problems. Her work shows that at the start of life itself the individual is in contact with the breast and, by rapid extension of primitive awareness, with the family group; furthermore she has shown that the nature of this contact displays qualities peculiar to itself, which are of profound significance both in the development of the individual and for a fuller understanding of the mechanisms already demonstrated by the intuitive genius of Freud.

I hope to show that in his contact with the complexities of life in a group the adult resorts, in what may be a massive regression, to mechanisms described by Melanie Klein (1931, 1946) as typical of the earliest phases of mental life. The adult must establish contact with the emotional life of the group in which he lives; this task would appear to be as formidable to the adult as the relationship with the breast

---

[1] Notably in *Totem and Taboo* (1913) and *Group Psychology and the Analysis of the Ego* (1921).

appears to be to the infant, and the failure to meet the demands of this task is revealed in his regression. The belief that a group exists, as distinct from an aggregate of individuals, is an essential part of this regression, as are also the characteristics with which the supposed group is endowed by the individual. Substance is given to the phantasy that the group exists by the fact that the regression involves the individual in a loss of his 'individual distinctiveness' (Freud, 1921, p. 9), indistinguishable from depersonalization, and therefore obscures observation that the aggregation is of individuals. It follows that if the observer judges a group to be in existence, the individuals composing it must have experienced this regression. Conversely, should the individuals composing a 'group' (using that word to mean an aggregation of individuals all in the same state of regression) for some reason or other becomes threatened by awareness of their individual distinctiveness, then the group is in the emotional state known as panic. This does not mean that the group is disintegrating, and it will be seen later that I do not agree that in panic the group has lost its cohesiveness.

In this paper I shall summarize certain theories at which I have arrived by applying in groups the intuitions developed by present-day psycho-analytic training. These theories differ from many others, in merits and defects alike, in being educed in the situations of emotional stress that they are intended to describe. I introduce some concepts new to psycho-analysis, partly because I deal with different subject matter, partly because I wanted to see if a start disencumbered by previous theories might lead to a point at which my views of the group and psycho-analytic views of the individual could be compared, and thereby judged to be either complementary or divergent.

There are times when I think that the group has an attitude to me, and that I can state in words what the attitude is;

there are times when another individual acts as if he also thought the group had an attitude to him, and I believe I can deduce what his belief is; there are times when I think that the group has an attitude to an individual, and that I can say what it is. These occasions provide the raw material on which interpretations are based, but the interpretation itself is an attempt to translate into precise speech what I suppose to be the attitude of the group to me or to some other individual, and of the individual to the group. Only some of these occasions are used by me; I judge the occasion to be ripe for an interpretation when the interpretation would seem to be both obvious and unobserved.

The groups in which I have attempted to fill this role pass through a series of complex emotional episodes that permit the deduction of theories of group dynamics that I have found useful both in the illumination of what is taking place and in the exposure of nuclei of further developments. What follows is a summary of these theories.

THE WORK GROUP

In any group there may be discerned trends of mental activity. Every group, however casual, meets to 'do' something; in this activity, according to the capacities of the individuals, they co-operate. This co-operation is voluntary and depends on some degree of sophisticated skill in the individual. Participation in this activity is possible only to individuals with years of training and a capacity for experience that has permitted them to develop mentally. Since this activity is geared to a task, it is related to reality, its methods are rational, and, therefore, in however embryonic a form, scientific. Its characteristics are similar to those attributed by Freud (1911) to the ego. This facet of mental activity in a group I have called the Work Group. The term embraces only mental activity of a particular kind, not the people who indulge in it.

When patients meet for a group-therapy session it can always be seen that some mental activity is directed to the solution of the problems for which the individuals seek help. Here is an example of a passing phase in such a group:

Six patients and I are seated round a small room. Miss A suggests that it would be a good idea if members agreed to call each other by their Christian names.[1] There is some relief that a topic has been broached, glances are exchanged, and a flicker of synthetic animation is momentarily visible. Mr. B ventures that it is a good idea, and Mr. C says it would 'make things more friendly'. Miss A is encouraged to divulge her name but is forestalled by Miss D who says she does not like her Christian name and would rather it were not known. Mr. E suggests pseudonyms; Miss F examines her fingernails. Within a few minutes of Miss A's suggestion, the discussion has languished, and its place has been taken by furtive glances, an increasing number of which are directed towards me. Mr. B rouses himself to say that we must call each other something. The mood is now a compound of anxiety and increasing frustration. Long before I am mentioned it is clear that my name has become a preoccupation of the group. Left to its own devices the group promises to pass into apathy and silence.

For my present purposes I shall display such aspects of the episode as illustrate my use of the term work group. In the group itself I might well do the same, but that would depend on my assessment of the significance of the episode in the context of the group mental life, as far as it had then emerged.

---

[1] See also the discussion of taboo on names in *Totem and Taboo* (Freud, 1913, p. 54).

First, it is clear that if seven people are to talk together it would help the discussion if names were available. In so far as the discussion has arisen through awareness of that fact it is a product of work-group activity. But the group has gone further than to propose a step that would be helpful in any group no matter what its task might be. The proposal has been made that Christian names should be used because that would make for friendliness. In the group of which I am speaking it would have been accurate to say that the production of friendliness was regarded as strictly relevant to therapeutic need. At the point in its history from which the example is taken, it would also be true to say that both Miss D's objection and Mr. E's proposed solution would be regarded as dictated by therapeutic need; and in fact I pointed out that the suggestions fitted in with a theory, not yet explicitly stated, that our diseases would be cured if the group could be conducted in such a way that only pleasant emotions were experienced. It will be seen that the demonstration of work-group function must include: the development of thought designed for translation into action; the theory, in this instance the need for friendliness, on which it is based; the belief in environmental change as in itself sufficient for cure without any corresponding change in the individual; and finally a demonstration of the kind of fact that is believed to be 'real'.

It so happened, in the instance I have given, that I was subsequently able to demonstrate that work-group function, though I did not call it that, based on the idea that cure could be obtained from a group in which pleasant feelings only were experienced, did not appear to have produced the hoped-for cure; and indeed was being obstructed by some sort of difficulty in achieving a limited translation into the apparently simple act of assigning names. Before passing to the discussion of the nature of the obstructions to work-

10

group activity, I would mention here a difficulty, which must already be evident, in the exposition of my theories. For me to describe a group episode, such as the one I have been discussing, and then to attempt the deduction of theories from it, is only to say that I have a theory that such-and-such took place and that I can say it again only in different language. The only way in which the reader can deliver himself from the dilemma is to recall to himself the memory of some committee or other gathering in which he has participated and consider to what extent he can recall evidence that could point to the existence of what I call work-group function, not forgetting the actual administrative structure, chairman and so forth, as material to be included in his review.

THE BASIC ASSUMPTIONS

The interpretations in terms of work-group activity leave much unsaid; is the suggested use of pseudonyms motivated only with a view to meeting the demands of reality? The furtive glances, the preoccupation with the correct mode for addressing the analyst, which became quite overt subsequently, cannot profitably be interpreted as related to work-group function.

Work-group activity is obstructed, diverted, and on occasion assisted, by certain other mental activities that have in common the attribute of powerful emotional drives. These activities, at first sight chaotic, are given a certain cohesion if it is assumed they spring from basic assumptions common to all the group. In the example I have given it was easy to recognize that one assumption common to all the group was that they were met together to receive some form of treatment from me. But exploration of this idea as part of work-group function showed that ideas existed invested with reality by force of the emotion attached to them, that were not in conformity even with the somewhat naïve expectation consciously entertained by the less sophisticated members. Furthermore, even sophisticated individuals, one member for example being a graduate in science, showed by their behaviour that they shared these ideas.

The first assumption is that the group is met in order to be sustained by a leader on whom it depends for nourishment, material and spiritual, and protection. Stated thus, my first basic assumption might be regarded as a repetition of my remark, above, that the group assumed that 'they were met together to receive some form of treatment from me', only differing from it in being couched in metaphorical terms. But the essential point is that the basic assumption can only be understood if the words in which I have stated it are taken as literal and not metaphorical.

Here is a description of a therapeutic group in which the dependent assumption, as I shall call it, is active.

Three women and two men were present. The group had on a previous occasion shown signs of work-group function directed towards curing the disability of its members; on this occasion they might be supposed to have reacted from this with despair, placing all their reliance on me to sort out their difficulties while they contented themselves with in- dividually posing questions to which I was to provide the answers. One woman had brought some chocolate, which she diffidently invited her right-hand neighbour, another woman, to share. One man was eating a sandwich. A graduate in philosophy, who had in earlier sessions told the group he had no belief in God, and no religion, sat silent, as indeed he often did, until one of the women with a touch of acerbity in her tone, remarked that he had asked no questions. He replied, 'I do not need to talk because I know that I only have to come here long enough and all my

questions will be answered without my having to do anything.'

I then said that I had become a kind of group deity; that
the questions were directed to me as one who knew the
answers without need to resort to work, that the eating was
part of a manipulation of the group to give substance to a
belief they wished to preserve about me, and that the
philosopher's reply indicated a disbelief in the efficacy of
prayer but seemed otherwise to belie earlier statements he
had made about his disbelief in God. When I began my interpretation I was not only convinced of its truth but felt no
doubt that I could convince the others by confrontation with
the mass of material—only some of which I can convey in
this printed account. By the time I had finished speaking I
felt I had committed some kind of gaffe; I was surrounded
by blank looks; the evidence had disappeared. After a time,
the man, who had finished his sandwich and placed the carefully folded paper in his pocket, looked round the room, eye-
brows slightly raised, interrogation in his glance. A woman
looked tensely at me, another with hands folded gazed
meditatively at the floor. In me a conviction began to harden
that I had been guilty of blasphemy in a group of true be-
lievers. The second man, with elbow draped over the back of
his chair, played with his fingers. The woman who was eating, hurriedly swallowed the last of her chocolate. I now
interpreted that I had become a very bad person, casting
doubts on the group deity, but that this had been followed by
an increase of anxiety and guilt as the group had failed to
dissociate itself from the impiety.

In this account I have dwelt on my own reactions in the
group for a reason which I hope may become more apparent
later. It can be justly argued that interpretations for which
the strongest evidence lies, not in the observed facts in the
group but in the subjective reactions of the analyst, are more

likely to find their explanation in the psychopathology of the analyst than in the dynamics of the group. It is a just criticism, and one which will have to be met by years of careful work by more than one analyst, but for that very reason I shall leave it on one side and pass on to state now a contention that I shall support throughout this paper. It is that in group treatment many interpretations, and amongst them the most important, have to be made on the strength of the analyst's own emotional reactions. It is my belief that these reactions are dependent on the fact that the analyst in the group is at the receiving end of what Melanie Klein (1946) has called projective identification, and that this mechanism plays a very important role in groups. Now the experience of counter-transference appears to me to have quite a distinct quality that should enable the analyst to differentiate the occasion when he is the object of a projective identification from the occasion when he is not. The analyst feels he is being manipulated so as to be playing a part, no matter how difficult to recognize, in somebody else's phantasy—or he would do if it were not for what in recollection I can only call a temporary loss of insight, a sense of experiencing strong feelings and at the same time a belief that their existence is quite adequately justified by the objective situation without recourse to recondite explanation of their causation. From the analyst's point of view, the experience consists of two closely related phases: in the first there is a feeling that whatever else one has done, one has certainly not given a correct interpretation; in the second there is a sense of being a particular kind of person in a particular emotional situation. I believe ability to shake oneself out of the numbing feeling of reality that is a concomitant of this state is the prime requisite of the analyst in the group: if he can do this he is in a position to give what I believe is the correct interpretation, and thereby to see its connection with the previous interpretation, the validity of which he has been caused to doubt.

I must return to consider the second basic assumption. Like the first, this also concerns the purpose for which the group has met. My attention was first aroused by a session in which the conversation was monopolized by a man and woman who appeared more or less to ignore the rest of the group. The occasional exchange of glances amongst the others seemed to suggest the view, not very seriously entertained, that the relationship was amatory, although one would hardly say that the overt content of the conversation was very different from other interchanges in the group. I was, however, impressed with the fact that individuals, who were usually sensitive to any exclusion from supposedly therapeutic activity, which at that time had come to mean talking and obtaining an 'interpretation' from me or some other member of the group, seemed not to mind leaving the stage entirely to this pair. Later it became clear that the sex of the pair was of no particular consequence to the assumption that pairing was taking place. There was a peculiar air of hopefulness and expectation about these sessions which made them rather different from the usual run of hours of boredom and frustration. It must not be supposed that the elements to which I would draw attention, under the title of pairing group, are exclusively or even predominantly in evidence. In fact there is plenty of evidence of states of mind of the kind we are familiar with in psycho-analysis; it would indeed be extraordinary, to take one example, if one did not see in individuals evidence of reaction to a group situation that could approximate to an acting out of the primal scene. But, in my opinion, to allow one's attention to be absorbed by these reactions is to make difficult any observation of what is peculiar to the group; furthermore I think such concentration at worst can lead to a debased psycho-analysis rather than an exploration of the therapeutic possibilities of the group. The reader must, then, assume that in this, as in other situations, there will always be a plethora of material familiar in a psycho-analysis, but still awaiting its evaluation in the situation of the group; this material I propose for the present to ignore, and I shall now turn to a consideration of the air of hopeful expectation that I have mentioned as a characteristic of the pairing group. It usually finds expression verbally in ideas that marriage would put an end to neurotic disabilities; that group therapy would revolutionize society when it had spread sufficiently; that the coming season, spring, summer, autumn, or winter, as the case may be, will be more agreeable; that some new kind of community—an improved group—should be developed, and so on. These expressions tend to divert attention to some supposedly future event, but for the analyst the crux is not a future event but the immediate present—the feeling of hope itself. This feeling is characteristic of the pairing group and must be taken by itself as evidence that the pairing group is in existence, even when other evidence appears to be lacking. It is itself both a precursor of sexuality and a part of it. The optimistic ideas that are verbally expressed are rationalizations intended to effect a displacement in time and a compromise with feelings of guilt—the enjoyment of the feeling is justified by appeal to an outcome supposedly morally unexceptionable. The feelings thus associated in the pairing group are at the opposite pole to feelings of hatred, destructiveness, and despair. For the feelings of hope to be sustained it is essential that the 'leader' of the group, unlike the leader of the dependent group and of the fight-flight group, should be unborn. It is a person or idea that will save the group—in fact from feelings of hatred, destructiveness, and despair, of its own or of another group—but in order to do this, obviously, the Messianic hope must never be fulfilled. Only by remaining a hope does hope persist. The difficulty is that, thanks to the rationalization of the dawning sexuality of the group, the premonition of sex which obtrudes as hope, there is a tendency for the work group to be influenced in the direction of producing a Messiah, be it person, idea, or Utopia. In so far as it succeeds, hope is weakened; for obviously nothing is then to hope for, and, since destructiveness, hatred, and despair have in no way been radically influenced, their existence again makes itself felt. This in turn accelerates a further weakening of hope. If, for purposes of discussion, we accept the idea that the group should be manipulated in order to compass hopefulness in the group, then it is necessary that those who concern themselves with such a task, either in their capacity as members of a specialized work group such as I shall describe shortly, or as individuals, should see to it that Messianic hopes do not materialize. The danger, of course, is that such specialized work groups will either suffer through excess of zeal and thereby interfere with innocent, creative work-group function or alternatively allow themselves to be forestalled and so put to the troublesome necessity of liquidating the Messiah and then recreating the Messianic hope. In the therapeutic group the problem is to enable the group to be consciously aware of the feelings of hope, and its affiliations, and at the same time tolerant of them. That it is tolerant of them in the pairing group is a function of the basic assumption and cannot be regarded as a sign of individual development.

The third basic assumption is that the group has met to fight something or to run away from it. It is prepared to do either indifferently. I call this state of mind the fight-flight group; the accepted leader of a group in this state is one whose demands on the group are felt to afford opportunity for flight or aggression and if he makes demands that do not do so, he is ignored. In a therapeutic group the analyst is the work-group leader. The emotional backing that he can command is subject to fluctuation according to the active basic assumption and the extent to which his activities are felt to fit in with what is required of a leader in these differing states of mind. In the fight-flight group the analyst finds that attempts to illuminate what is taking place are obstructed by the ease with which emotional support is obtained for such proposals as express either hatred of all psychological difficulty or alternatively the means by which it can be evaded. In this context I would remark that the proposal to use Christian names, in the first example I gave, might well have been interpreted as an expression of the desire for flight in a fight-flight group though, in fact, for reasons connected with the stage of development that the group had reached, I interpreted it in terms of work-group function.

CHARACTERISTICS COMMON TO ALL BASIC-ASSUMPTION GROUPS

Participation in basic-assumption activity requires no training, experience, or mental development. It is instantaneous, inevitable, and instinctive: I have not felt the need to postulate the existence of a herd instinct to account for such phenomena as I have witnessed in the group.[1] In contrast with work-group function basic-assumption activity makes no demands on the individual for a capacity to co-operate but depends on the individual's possession of what I call valency —a term I borrow from the physicists to express a capacity for instantaneous involuntary combination of one individual with another for sharing and acting on a basic assumption.

[1] In contrast with W. Trotter (1916) but in agreement with Freud (1921, p. 3).

Work-group function is always in evidence with one, and only one, basic assumption. Though the work-group function may remain unaltered, the contemporary basic assumption that pervades its activities can be changing frequently; there may be two or three changes in an hour or the same basic assumption may be dominant for months on end. To account for the fate of the inactive basic assumptions I have postulated the existence of a proto-mental system in which physical and mental activity is undifferentiated, and which lies outside the field ordinarily considered profitable for psychological investigations. It must be borne in mind that the question whether a field is suitable for psychological investigation depends on other factors besides the nature of the field to be investigated, one being the potency of the investigating psychological technique. The recognition of a field of psychosomatic medicine illustrates the difficulty that attends any attempt at determination of the line that separates psychological from physical phenomena. I propose therefore to leave indeterminate the limits that separate the active basic assumption from those I have relegated to the hypothetical proto-mental system.

Many techniques are in daily use for the investigation of work-group function. For the investigation of basic-assumption phenomena, I consider psycho-analysis, or some extension of technique derived directly from it, to be essential. But since work-group functions are always pervaded by basic-assumption phenomena it is clear that techniques that ignore the latter will give misleading impressions of the former.

Emotions associated with basic assumptions may be described by the usual terms, anxiety, fear, hate, love, and the like. But the emotions common to any basic assumption are subtly affected by each other as if they were held in a combination peculiar to the active basic assumption. That is to say, anxiety in the dependent group has a different quality from anxiety evident in the pairing group, and so on with other feelings.

All basic assumptions include the existence of a leader, although in the pairing group, as I have said, the leader is 'non-existent', i.e. unborn. This leader need not be identified with any individual in the group; it need not be a person at all but may be identified with an idea or an inanimate object. In the dependent group the place of leader may be filled by the history of the group. A group, complaining of an inability to remember what took place on a previous occasion, sets about making a record of its meetings. This record then becomes a 'bible' to which appeal is made, if, for example, the individual whom the group has invested with leadership proves to be refractory material for moulding into the likeness proper to the dependent leader. The group resorts to bible-making when threatened with an idea the acceptance of which would entail development on the part of the individuals comprising the group. Such ideas derive emotional force, and excite emotional opposition, from their association with characteristics appropriate to the pairing-group leader. When the dependent group or the fight-flight group is active, a struggle takes place to suppress the new idea because it is felt that the emergence of the new idea threatens the *status quo*. In war, the new idea—be it a tank or a new method for selecting officers—is felt to be 'new-fangled', i.e. opposed to the military bible. In the dependent group it is felt to threaten the dependent leader, be that leader 'bible' or person. But the same is true of the pairing-group, for here the new idea or person, being equated with the unborn genius or Messiah, must, as I have said before, remain unborn if it, or he, is to fulfil the pairing-group function.

ABERRANT FORMS OF CHANGE FROM ONE BASIC ASSUMPTION TO ANOTHER

Change in the mentality of the group need not be due to the displacement of one basic assumption by another and can take certain aberrant forms which depend on what basic assumption is active when tension increases. These aberrant forms always involve an extraneous group. If the dependent group is active, and is threatened by pressure of the pairing-group leader, particularly perhaps in the form of an idea which is suffused with Messianic hope, then if methods such as a resort to bible-making prove inadequate, the threat is countered by provoking the influx of another group. If the fight-flight group is active, the tendency is to absorb another group. If the pairing group is active, the tendency is to schism. This last reaction may appear anomalous unless it is remembered that in the pairing group the Messianic hope, be it person or idea, must remain unrealized. The crux of the matter lies in the threat of the new idea to demand development and the inability of the basic-assumption groups to tolerate development. The reasons for this I shall educe later.

THE SPECIALIZED WORK GROUP

There are certain specialized work groups, to which Freud (1921, pp. 41 f) has drawn attention though not under this name, whose task is peculiarly prone to stimulate the activity of a particular basic assumption. Typical groups of this nature are provided by a Church or an Army. A Church is liable to interference from dependent-group phenomena, and the Army suffers a similar liability from fight-flight group phenomena. But another possibility has to be considered, namely that these groups are budded off by the main group of which they form a part, for the specific purpose of neutralizing dependent group and fight-flight group respectively and thus preventing their obstruction of the work-group function of the main group. If we adopt the latter hypothesis, it must be regarded as a failure in the specialized work group if dependent or fight-flight group activity either ceases to manifest itself within the specialized work groups or else grows to overwhelming strength. In either case the result is the same—the main group has to take over the functions proper to the specialized work group, and yet fulfil its work-group functions. If the specialized work group cannot, or does not, cope with the basic-assumption phenomena that are its province, then the work-group functions of the main group are vitiated by the pressure of these basic assumptions. As work-group function consists essentially of the translation of thoughts and feelings into behaviour which is adapted to reality, it is ill-adapted to give expression to basic assumptions. For basic assumptions become dangerous in proportion as the attempt is made to translate them into action. Indeed, the specialized work group has tended to recognize this and shows it by the attempt to carry out the reverse process, namely to translate action into terms of basic-assumption mentality—a much safer proceeding. Thus, a Church, when presented with some notable achievement of work-group function, will adjure the group to give thanks to its deity and not to its capacity for realistic hard work, 'non nobis, Domine'. The prosperous and successful Church, from the point of view of easing work-group function, must combine fortification of religious belief with the insistence that it must never be acted on; the successful fighting service must encourage the belief that anything can be done by force provided always it is never used. In both cases it comes to this—basic-assumption mentality does not lend itself to translation into action, since action requires work-group function to maintain contact with reality.

In the small therapeutic group, the tendency, when the dependent group is active, is to produce a sub-group which then takes on the function of interpreting the dependent-group leader—usually located in the analyst—to the group. In the fight-flight group a similar sub-group fulfils a similar function. If the analyst proves obdurate material, he is liable to evoke reactions which I have already described as associated with the threat of the new idea.

I have mentioned above (p. 136) that an aristocracy may constitute the specialized work group that fulfils for the pairing group functions similar to those which Church or Army fulfil for the dependent and fight-flight groups respectively. The function of this sub-group is to provide an outlet for feelings centred on ideas of breeding and birth, that is to say for Messianic hope, which I have already suggested is a precursor to sexual desire, without ever arousing the fear that such feelings will give rise to an event that will demand development. The aristocracy must inspire Messianic hope but at the same time confidence that the pairing-group leader, if he materializes, will be born in a palace but be just like ourselves—'democratic' is probably the modern cant term for the desired quality. In the therapeutic group the 'aristocratic' sub-group usually helps the group to understand that the new idea is one with which they are already quite familiar.

BASIC ASSUMPTIONS, TIME, AND DEVELOPMENT

There are two characteristics of basic-assumption mentality to which I would draw attention. Time plays no part in it; it is a dimension of mental function that is not recognized; consequently all activities that require an awareness of time are imperfectly comprehended and tend to arouse feelings of persecution. Interpretations of activity on the level of the basic assumptions lay bare a disturbed relationship to time. The second characteristic, which I mentioned earlier, is the absence of any process of development as a part of basic assumption mentality; stimuli to development meet with a hostile response. It will be appreciated that this is a matter of importance in any group that purports, by the study of the group, to promote a therapeutic development of insight. Hostility thus engendered tends to determine that the re-action to the emergence of the Messianic person or idea will take an aberrant form rather than spend itself in the cyclic change from one basic assumption to another. For, if a group wishes to prevent development, the simplest way to do so is to allow itself to be overwhelmed by basic-assumption men-tality and thus become approximated to the one kind of mental life in which a capacity for development is not re-quired. The main compensation for such a shift appears to be an increase in a pleasurable feeling of vitality.

The defence that schism affords against the development-threatening idea can be seen in the operation of the schis-matic groups, ostensibly opposed but in fact promoting the same end. One group adheres to the dependent group, often in the form of the group 'bible'. This group popularizes the established ideas by denuding them of any quality that might demand painful effort and thereby secures a numerous ad-herence of those who oppose the pains of development. Thought thus becomes stabilized on a level that is platitud-inous and dogmatic. The reciprocal group, supposedly sup-porting the new idea, becomes so exacting in its demands that it ceases to recruit itself. Thus both groups avoid the painful bringing together of the primitive and the sophisti-cated that is the essence of the developmental conflict. The superficial but numerous schismatics are thus opposed by the profound but numerically negligible schismatics. The result reminds one of the fear expressed sometimes that a society breeds copiously from its least cultural members while the 'best' people remain obdurately sterile.

RELATION OF ONE BASIC ASSUMPTION TO ANOTHER

We may now reconsider the three basic-assumption groups and the work group to see if they are not capable of resolution into something more fundamental. Granting that the postulate of basic assumptions helps to give form and meaning to the complex and chaotic emotional state that the group unfolds to the investigating participant, there is yet no reasonable explanation of why such assumptions should exist. It is clear that no one of the three basic assumptions about the group satisfactorily allays fear of the group and its emotions, otherwise there would be none of the shifts and changes from one to another and no need for the formation, which I have sketched out, of the corresponding specialized work groups. All three basic assumptions contain the idea of a leader. The fight-flight group shows a total absence of recognition of understanding as a technique. All are opposed to development, which is itself dependent on understanding. The work group, on the other hand, recognizes a need both to understand and to develop. If we consider the specialized work groups, all three are concerned with matters that appear to lie outside the province of the basic assumption with which they appear primarily to be concerned. Thus the specialized work group of the dependent basic assumption is not free from preoccupation with Messianic ideas that appear to be more in the sphere of pairing-group activity than of the dependent group. Effort here seems to be devoted to a Messiah born, out of wedlock, in a bed of bulrushes or a manger, with one exalted parent, Pharaoh's daughter or the Deity, and one less exalted. In the pairing group the aristocratic sub-group allows exalted parents, wedlock, and a palatial crib, but the child is notable only in being one with the rest of us. A scrutiny of the facts seems to lead to a central difficulty in bringing together sexual love, equal parents, an infant like ourselves, the Messianic hope which I consider to be an essential component of the sexual love, and a compulsion to develop that in itself necessitates a capacity for understanding. The fight-flight group expresses a sense of incapacity for understanding and the love without which understanding cannot exist. But the leader of the fight-flight group brings back into view one of the feared components, an approximation either to the dreaded father or the infant.

Furthermore, the three basic-assumption groups seem each in turn to be aggregates of individuals sharing out between them the characteristics of one character in the Œdipal situation, which are depending on whichever basic assumption is active. The parallel with the characters in the Œdipal situation is however marked by important divergences. The relationship appears to be between the individual and the group. But the group is felt as one fragmented individual with another, hidden, in attendance. The hidden individual is the leader, and although this appears to contradict the constantly reiterated statement that the analyst is the leader, the contradiction is resolved if it is remembered that in the therapeutic group the analyst is the work-group leader, and if attention is paid to the many indications that he is suspected of leading, but apparently only rarely perceived to be leading. It is quite common, in my experience, to be told I am not taking any part in the group or ever giving the group a chance to know what my views are, although the probability is that I am doing more talking than anyone else. The essential point here, as always in a group, is the feeling with which the idea expressed is accompanied, and the point I would emphasize again is that I am suspected of, but not perceived to be, leading the group.

11

On the emotional plane, where basic assumptions are dominant, Œdipal figures, as I have indicated, can be discerned in the material just as they are in a psycho-analysis. But they include one component of the Œdipus myth of which little has been said, and that is the sphinx. In so far as I am felt to be leader of work-group function, and recognition of that fact is seldom absent, I, and the work-group function with which I am identified, am invested with feelings that would be quite appropriate to the enigmatic, brooding, and questioning sphinx from whom disaster emanates. In fact terms are sometimes employed, on occasions when my intervention has provoked more than usual anxiety, which hardly require interpretation to enable the group to grasp the similarity. I know of no experience that demonstrates more clearly than the group experience the dread with which a questioning attitude is regarded. This anxiety is not directed only towards the questoner but also to the object of the inquiry and is, I suspect, secondary to the latter. For the group, as being the object of inquiry, itself arouses fears of an extremely primitive kind. My impression is that the group approximates too closely, in the minds of the individuals composing it, to very primitive phantasies about the contents of the mother's body.[1] The attempt to make a rational investigation of the dynamics of the group is therefore perturbed by fears, and mechanisms for dealing with them, that are characteristic of the paranoid-schizoid position. The investigation cannot be carried out without the stimulation and activation of these levels.

We are now in a better position to consider whether the basic assumptions are capable of resolution into something more fundamental. I have drawn attention already to the fact that these three states of mind have resemblances to

---

[1] Melanie Klein.

each other that would lead me to suppose that they may not be fundamental phenomena, but rather expressions of, or reactions against, some state more worthy of being regarded as primary. In fact, although I have found the hypothesis of basic assumptions a valuable aid in producing order out of the chaos of material in a group session, it is soon clear that further investigation demands fresh hypotheses. The need, and the way to the hypothesis that might satisfy it, became apparent to me in considering what could precipitate the change from one basic assumption to another. I include in this discussion the aberrant forms I have already described.

In brief, no matter what basic assumption is active, investigation discloses that the elements in the emotional situation are so closely allied to phantasies of the earlier anxieties that the group is compelled, whenever the pressure of anxiety becomes too great, to take defensive action. Approached from this primitive level, the basic assumptions take on a different aspect from that which they present in the descriptions I have already given. The impulse to pair may now be seen to possess a component derived from psychotic anxiety associated with primitive Œdipal conflicts working on a foundation of part-object relationships. This anxiety compels individuals to seek allies. This derivation of the impulse to pair is cloaked by the apparently rational explanation in the pairing group that the motive is sexual and the object reproduction.

But if the pairing group is active, again we find that many of its components are too close to primitive part objects to escape identification with them so that it is only a matter of time before psychotic anxiety is aroused with such force that new defence must be found. Let us suppose that it takes the form of the fight-flight group, that is to say the release of hate which finds an outlet either in destructive attacks on a supposed enemy or flight from the hated object. The indifference of the group to the individual, and still more the inability of the group to escape by this means from the primitive primal scene, again leads to release of anxiety and the need for another change of basic assumption.

It will be seen from this description that the basic assumptions now emerge as formations secondary to an extremely early primal scene worked out on a level of part objects, and associated with psychotic anxiety and mechanisms of splitting and projective identification such as Melanie Klein has described as characteristic of the paranoid-schizoid and depressive positions. Introjection and projection of the group,[1] which is now the feared investigator, now the feared object of investigation, form an essential part of the picture and help to add confusion to the scene unless recognized as being very active.

The classical view of the primal scene does not go far enough to deal with the dynamics of the group. I must stress the point that I consider it essential to work out very thoroughly the primitive primal scene as it discloses itself in the group. This differs markedly from the primal scene in its classical description in that it is much more bizarre and seems to assume that a part of one parent, the breast or the mother's body, contains amongst other objects a part of the father. In her paper on early stages of the Œdipus conflict, Melanie Klein (1928; also 1945) gives a description of these phantasies as she discovered them in the process of individual analysis (see Paula Heimann, 1952b). The group experience seems to me to give ample material to support the view that these phantasies are of paramount importance for the group.[2]

---

[1] How this appears in psycho-analysis is described by Paula Heimann (1952a).

[2] It is worth noting that Melanie Klein's description of the psychotic reaction to external objects in her paper on 'Early Stages of the Œdipus Conflict' (1928) is markedly similar to the group's reaction to ideas. Bible-making is one form of defence against them.

The more disturbed the group, the more easily discernible are these primitive phantasies and mechanisms; the more stable the group, the more it corresponds with Freud's description of the group as a repetition of family group patterns and neurotic mechanisms. But even in the 'stable' group the deep psychotic levels should be demonstrated, though it may involve temporarily an apparent increase in the 'illness' of the group.

SUMMARY

Before turning to discuss psycho-analytic views of the group, I think it is necessary to sum up the theories I have described so far. It will be remembered that I attempted deliberately, in so far as it is possible to a psycho-analyst admittedly proposing to investigate the group through psycho-analytically developed intuitions, to divest myself of any earlier psycho-analytic theories of the group in order to achieve an unprejudiced view. In the result I have arrived at a theory of the group as giving evidence of work-group functions together with behaviour, often strongly emotionally coloured, which suggested that groups were reacting emotionally to one of three basic assumptions. The idea that such basic assumptions are made involuntarily, automatically, inevitably has seemed useful in illuminating the behaviour of the group. Nevertheless, there is much to suggest that these supposed 'basic assumptions' cannot be regarded as distinct states of mind. By that I do not mean to claim that they are 'basic' explanations which between them explain all conduct in the group—that would indeed be extravagant nonsense—but that each state, even when it is possible to differentiate it with reasonable certainty from the other two, has about it a quality that suggests it may in some way be the dual, or reciprocal of one of the other two, or perhaps simply another view of what one had thought to be a different basic assumption. For example, the Messianic hope of the pairing group has some similarity to the group deity of the dependent group. It may be difficult to see because the presenting emotional tone is so different. Anxiety, fear, hate, love, all, as I have said, exist in each basic-assumption group. The modification that feelings suffer in combination in the respective basic-assumption group may arise because the 'cement', so to speak, that joined them to each other is guilt and depression in the dependent group, Messianic hope in the pairing group, anger and hate in the fight-flight group. Be that as it may, the result is that the thought content of the discussion may appear as a result to be deceptively different in the three groups. It is possible at times to feel that the unborn genius of the pairing group is very similar to the god of the dependent group; certainly on those occasions when the dependent group appeals to the authority of a 'past' leader it comes very close to the pairing group, which appeals to a 'future' leader. In both the leader does not exist; there is a difference of tense and a difference in emotion.

I retiterate these points to show that the hypothesis of the basic assumptions that I have put forward cannot be regarded as a rigid formulation.

THE PSYCHO-ANALYTIC VIEW

Freud's theories of the group derive from his study of the transference. Since the pair relationship of psycho-analysis can be regarded as a part of the larger group situation, the transference relationship could be expected, for the reasons I have already given, to be coloured by the characteristics associated with the pairing group. If analysis is regarded as part of the total group situation, we should expect to find sexual elements prominent in the material there presented, and the suspicions and hostilities of psycho-analysis as a sexual activity active in that part of the group which is in fact excluded from the analysis.

From his experience of analysis Freud was able to deduce the significance of two of what I have called specialized work groups, Army and Church, but did not discuss the specialized work group that attaches most importance to breeding, and is therefore most likely to have to deal with pairing-group phenomena, namely the aristocracy. If the aristocracy were concerned simply with the external reality, its activity would far more closely resemble the work of a genetics department in a university than it does. But the interest shown in breeding has not the scientific aura we should associate with mental activity directed to external reality: it is a specialized work group split off to deal with pairing-group phenomena in much the same way as the army has to deal with fight-flight phenomena and the Church with dependent-group phenomena. Therefore, the relationship of this sub-group with the main group will not be determined by the degree of fidelity to the strict genetic principles with which it conducts its affairs but rather by the efficiency with which it satisfies the main-group demand that pairing-group phenomena are dealt with so that work-group functions of the total group are not obstructed by emotional drives from that source. Although he expressly disavowed any but a superficial study of the group problem (1913, pp. 75 ff), and made his observations in the course of a discussion of the views of Le Bon, Mc-Dougall, and Wilfred Trotter, Freud (1921, passim) in fact had ample experience of the group and what it means to be an individual caught up in its emotional stresses—as I have indicated by my picture of the position psycho-analysis is likely to occupy in a group in which it stimulates a pairing group.

Freud (1930, pp. 44 ff) says individual and group psychology cannot be absolutely differentiated because the psychology of the individual is itself a function of the relationship between one person and another. He objects that it is difficult to attribute to number a significance so great as to make it capable by itself of arousing in our mental life a new instinct that is otherwise not brought into play. In this view I think Freud right; I have not at any time met with any phenomena that require explanation by a postulation of a herd instinct. The individual is, and always has been, a member of a group, even if his membership of it consists of behaving in such a way that reality is given to an idea that he does not belong to a group at all. The individual is a group animal at war, both with the group and with those aspects of his personality that constitute his 'groupishness'. Freud (1921, p. 29) limits this war to a struggle with 'culture', but I hope to show that this requires further expansion.

McDougall and Le Bon seem to speak as if group psychology comes into being only when a number of people are collected together in one place at one time, and Freud does not disavow this. For my part this is not necessary except to make study possible: the aggregation of individuals is only necessary in the way that it is necessary for analyst and analysed to come together for the transference relationship to be demonstrable. Only by coming together are adequate conditions provided for the demonstration of the characteristics of the group; only if individuals come sufficiently close to each other is it possible to give an interpretation without shouting it; equally, it is necessary for all members of the group to be able to witness the evidence on which interpretations are based. For these reasons the numbers of the group, and the degree of dispersion, must be limited. The congregation of the group in a particular place at a particular time is, for these mechanical reasons, important, but it has no significance for the production of group phenomena; the idea that it has springs from the impression that a thing must commence at the moment when its existence becomes demonstrable. In fact no individual, however isolated in time and space, should be regarded as outside a group or lacking in active manifestations of group psychology. Nevertheless, the existence of group behaviour is, as I say, clearly more easy to demonstrate, and even to observe, if the group is brought together; and I think it is this increased ease of observation and demonstration that is responsible for the idea of a herd instinct, such as Trotter postulates, or of the various other theories I have already mentioned which amount in the end to the idea that a group is more than the sum of its members. My experience convinces me that Freud was right to reject any such concept as, on present evidence, unnecessary. The apparent difference between group psychology and individual psychology is an illusion produced by the fact that the group brings into prominence phenomena that appear alien to an observer unaccustomed to using the group.[1,2]

I attribute great force and influence to the work group, which, through its concern with reality, is compelled to employ the methods of science in no matter how rudimentary a form; despite the influence of the basic assumptions, and sometimes in harmony with them, it is the work group that triumphs in the long run. Le Bon said that the group never thirsts after the truth. I agree with Freud's opinion—given particularly in discussing the part played by the group in the production of language,[3] folk-song, folk-lore, etc.—that in

---

[1] See discussion of these points on pp. 131 *et seq.*

[2] It is also a matter of historical development; there are aspects of group behaviour which appear strange unless there is some understanding of Melanie Klein's work on the psychoses. See particularly papers on symbol formation and schizoid mechanisms. I develop this point later.

[3] Later in this paper I discuss one aspect of the development of language.

saying this Le Bon is unfair to the group. When McDougall says that conditions in the highly organized group remove 'the psychological disadvantages of group formation' he approximates to my view that the function of the specialized work group is to manipulate the basic assumption so as to prevent obstruction of the work group. Freud describes the problem as one of procuring for the group 'precisely those features that were characteristic of the individual and are extinguished in him by the formation of the group'. He postulates an individual outside the primitive group who possessed his own continuity, his self-consciousness, his traditions and customs, his own particular functions and position. He says that, owing to his entry into an 'unorganized' group, the individual had lost his distinctiveness for a time. I think the struggle of the individual to preserve his distinctiveness assumes different characteristics according to the state of mind of the group at any given moment. Group organization gives stability and permanence to the work group, which is felt to be more easily submerged by the basic assumptions if the group is unorganized. Individual distinctiveness is no part of life in a group that is acting on the basic assumptions. Organization and structure are weapons of the work group. They are the product of co-operation between members of the group, and their effect, once established in the group, is to demand still further co-operation from the individuals in the group. In this respect McDougall's organized group is always a work group and never a basic-assumption group. A group acting on basic assumption would need neither organization nor a capacity for co-operation. The counterpart of co-operation in the basic-assumption group is valency—a spontaneous, unconscious function of the gregarious quality in the personality of man. It is only when a group begins to act on a basic assumption that difficulties arise. Action inevitably means contact with reality, and contact with reality compels regard for truth; scientific method is imposed, and the evocation of the work group follows. Le Bon described the leader as one under whom a collection of human beings instinctively place themselves, accepting his authority as their chief; the leader must fit in with the group in his personal qualities and must himself be held by a strong faith in order to awaken the group's faith. His view of the leader as one who must fit in with the group in his personal qualities is compatible with my view that any leader is ignored by the group when his behaviour or characteristics fall outside the limits set by the prevalent basic assumption. Further, the leader must be held by the same 'faith' that holds the group—not in order to awaken the group's faith but because the attitude of group and leader alike are functions of the active basic assumption.

McDougall's (1920, p. 45) distinction between the simple 'unorganized' group and the 'organized' group seems to me to apply, not to two different groups but to two states of mind that can be observed to co-exist in the same group. The 'organized' group, for reasons I have already given, is likely to display the characteristic features of the work group; the 'unorganized' of the basic-assumption group. Freud discusses McDougall's views, quoting his description of the 'unorganized' group. With regard to the suggestibility of the group, I think it depends what the suggestion is. If it falls within the terms of the active basic assumption, the group will follow it, if it does not, the group will ignore it. This characteristic seems to me to come out very clearly in panic, to which I refer later.

McDougall, discussed by Freud in the above-mentioned passage, draws up certain conditions for raising the level of collective mental life. 'The first of these conditions,' he says (1920, p. 49), 'which is the basis of all the rest, is some de-

gree of continuity of existence of the group.' This convinces
me that in the organized group McDougall is describing what
I call the work group. Meyer Fortes (1949), discussing Rad-
cliffe Brown's views on social structure, particularly the distinction between 'structure as an actually existing concrete
reality' and 'structural form', says that the distinction is
associated with the continuity of social structure through
time. In my view the continuity of social structure through
time is a function of the work group. Meyer Fortes states
that the time factor in social structure is by no means uniform
in its incidence and adds that all corporate groups, by
definition, must have continuity. As with McDougall's distinction between organized and unorganized groups, so with
the incidence of the time factor, I do not believe that we are
dealing with two different kinds of group, in the sense of two
different aggregates of individuals, but rather with two
different categories of mental activity co-existing in the same
group of individuals. In work-group activity time is intrinsic:
in basic assumption activity it has no place. Basic-assumption group functions are active before ever a group comes
together in a room, and continue after the group has dis-
persed. There is neither development nor decay in basic-
assumption functions, and in this respect they differ totally
from those of the work group. It is therefore to be expected
that observation of the group's continuity in time will produce anomalous and contradictory results if it has not been
recognized that two different kinds of mental functioning
operate within the group at the same time. The man who
asks, 'When does the group meet again?' is referring, in so
far as he is talking about mental phenomena, to work group.
The basic-assumption group does not disperse or meet, and
references to time have no meaning in the basic-assumption
group. I have known a group of intelligent men, to whom the
hours of the sessions were perfectly well known, express

anger because the session had ended, and to be quite unable for an appreciable time to grasp a fact that could not be a matter of doubt in work-group mentality. What is ordinarily called impatience must therefore, in the basic-assumption group, be considered as an expression of the anxiety which is aroused by phenomena intrinsically co-mingled with a dimension of which basic-assumption mentality knows nothing. It is as if a blind man were made aware of phenomena that could be understood only by one to whom the properties of light were familiar.

I would describe McDougall's principles for raising collective mental life to a higher level as an expression of the attempt to prevent obstruction of work group by basic-assumption group. His second condition stresses the need for the individual to have a clear view of the aims of the work group. His fourth point desiderates the existence of a body of traditions and customs and habits in the minds of the members of the group that will determine their relations to one another and to the group as a whole; this approximates to Plato's view that group harmony must be based on individual function and the firmness with which the individual is restricted to it. But it also has affinities with St. Augustine's view, in the 19th Book of *The City of God*, that a right relation with his fellows can only be achieved by a man who has first regulated his relationship with God. This may seem to contradict my statement that McDougall is concerned in his description of the organized group primarily with work-group phenomena. The difference between the two writers would seem to be this: McDougall is concerned to cope with basic assumptions by strengthening the work group's capacity to retain contact with external reality, while St. Augustine is elaborating a technique by which a specialized work group is formed with the specific function of maintaining contact with the basic assumption—in particular

with the dependent basic assumption. It is worth remembering that he was concerned to defend Christianity against the
charge of having so undermined morale that Rome had been
unable to resist the onslaught of Alaric. Put in other terms,
a body or group had arisen that was under suspicion of
having dealt with basic assumptions in a manner less efficient
than that of their pagan predecessors. St. Augustine is uneasily concerned to refute this. It is a predicament with which
those who purport to lead both public and group are not un-
familiar: the stimulation, and manipulation, of basic assumption, especially when done, as in some sort it must always
be done, without anything like adequate knowledge, or even
awareness, must lead to untoward results and sometimes even
to the dock.

I shall now consider that part of Freud's discussion which
turns on the statement that in a group an individual's
emotions become extraordinarily intensified, while his intellectual ability becomes markedly reduced. About this I
shall have something to say later when considering the group
from the point of view of the individual, but I wish for the
present to approach the matter, as Freud (1921, p. 33) does,
as a group phenomenon. In the groups I have studied it has
been natural for the group to expect me to take the lead in
organizing its activities. As I take advantage of the position
thus accorded me to lead the group in the direction of demonstrating group dynamics, the 'organization' of the group
does not do what McDougall says the organization of the
group is intended to do. The desire for an 'organized' group,
in McDougall's sense, is frustrated. Fear of the basic assumptions, which cannot be satisfactorily dealt with by structure
and organization, therefore expresses itself in the suppression of emotion, emotion being an essential part of the basic
assumptions. The tension thus produced appears to the individual as an intensification of emotion; the lack of structure

promotes the obtrusion of the basic-assumption group, and since in such a group the intellectual activity is, as I have already said, of an extremely limited kind, the individual, conforming with the behaviour imposed by participation in the basic-assumption group, feels as if his intellectual capacity were being reduced. The belief that this really is so is reinforced because the individual tends to ignore all intellectual activity that does not fit in with the basic assumption. In fact I do not in the least believe that there is a reduction of intellectual ability in the group, nor yet that 'great decisions in the realm of thought and momentous discoveries and solutions of problems are only possible to an individual working in solitude' (McDougall, 1920); although the belief that this is so is commonly expressed in the group discussion, and all sorts of plans are elaborated for circumventing the supposedly pernicious influence of the emotions of the group. Indeed I give interpretations because I believe that intellectual activity of a high order is possible in a group together with an awareness (and not an evasion) of the emotions of the basic-assumption groups. If group therapy is found to have a value, I believe it will be in the conscious experiencing of the group activity of this kind.

Freud turns to discussion of something that crops up under a variety of names, such as 'suggestion', 'imitation', 'prestige of leaders', 'contagion'. I have used 'valency' partly because I would avoid the meanings that already adhere to the terms I have listed, partly because the term 'valency', as used in physics to denote the power of combination of atoms, carries with it the greatest penumbra of suggestiveness useful for my purpose. By it I mean the capacity of the individual for instantaneous combination with other individuals in an established pattern of behaviour—the basic assumptions. Later I shall consider in greater detail what meaning we should attribute to this term when I am dealing with the psycho-analytic view of the individual's contribution.

I shall not follow Freud's discussion in detail, but will pass on to his use of the term 'libido', which he takes from his study of the psycho-neuroses (Freud, 1921). He thus approaches the group by way of psycho-analysis, and psycho-analysis, in the light of my experience of groups, can be regarded as a work group likely to stimulate the basic assumption of pairing; that being so, psycho-analytic investigation, as itself a part of pairing group, is likely to reveal sexuality in a central position. Further, it is likely to be attacked as itself a sexual activity since, according to my view of the pairing group, the group must assume that if two people come together, they can only do so for sexual purposes. It is therefore natural that Freud should see the nature of the bond between individuals in a group as libidinous. In the group, the libidinous component in the bond is characteristic of the pairing group, but I think it has a different complexion in the dependent group and the fight-flight group Freud describes the commander-in-chief of the Church as Christ, but I would say that it is the Deity. Christ, or the Messiah, is the leader, not of the dependent group but of the pairing group. In psycho-analysis, regarded as a part of the pairing group, the Messiah, or Messianic idea, occupies a central position, and the bond between individuals is libidinous. The Messianic idea betrays itself in the supposition that the individual patient is worth the analyst's very considerable devotion; as also in the view, sometimes openly expressed, that as a result of psycho-analytic work a technique will be perfected that will, ultimately, save mankind. In short, I regard Freud's use of the term libido as correct only for one phase, though an important one, and feel the need for some more neutral term that will describe the tie on all basic-assumption levels. The tie in the work group, which I regard as being a sophisticated nature, is more aptly described by the word co-operation.

Freud's notion of the leader as one on whom the group depends, and from whose personality it derives its qualities, seems to me to derive from his view of identification as almost entirely a process of introjection by the ego; to me the leader is as much the creature of the basic assumption as any other member of the group, and this, I think, is to be expected if we envisage identification of the individual with the leader as depending not on introjection alone but on a simultaneous process of projective identification (Melanie Klein, 1946) as well. The leader, on the basic-assumption level, does not create the group by virtue of his fanatical adherence to an idea, but is rather an individual whose personality renders him peculiarly susceptible to the obliteration of individuality by the basic-assumption group's leadership requirements. The 'loss of individual distinctiveness' applies to the leader of the group as much as to anyone else —a fact that probably accounts for some of the posturing to which leading figures are prone. Thus the leader in the fight-flight group, for example, appears to have a distinctive personality because his personality is of a kind that lends itself to exploitation by the group demand for a leader who requires of it only a capacity for fighting or for flight; the leader has no greater freedom to be himself than any other member of the group. It will be appreciated that this differs from Le Bon's idea that the leader must possess a strong and imposing will, and with Freud's idea that he corresponds to a hypnotist. Such power as he has derives from the fact that he has become, in common with every other member of the group, what Le Bon describes as 'an automaton who has ceased to be guided by his will'. In short, he is leader by virtue of his capacity for instantaneous, involuntary (maybe voluntary too) combination with every other member of his group, and only differs from them in that, whatever his

12

function in the work group, he is the incarnation of the basic-assumption-group leader.

Freud's view seems not to make explicit the dangerous possibilities that exist in the phenomenon of leadership. His view of the leader, and indeed all other views of which I am aware, is not easily reconciled with my experience of leadership as it emerges in practice. The leader of the work group at least has the merit of possessing contact with external reality, but no such qualification is required of the leader of the basic-assumption group. The usual description of the leader seems to be a mixture embodying various group phenomena, the characteristics of the work-group leader predominating. For reasons I have given, the work-group leader is either harmless through lack of influence with the group, or else a man whose grasp of reality is such that it carries authority. It is likely therefore that discussions of leadership coloured mostly by views of work-group-leader qualities will be optimistically tinged. My view of the basic-assumption-group leader does not rule out the possibility of identity with the work-group leader, but it allows for the existence of a leader apparently evoking the enthusiastic allegiance of the group, but devoid of contact with any reality other than the reality of the basic-assumption-group demands. When it is realized that this can mean that the group is being led by an individual whose qualification for the job is that his personality has been obliterated, an automaton, 'an individual who has lost his distinctiveness', but who yet is so suffused by the emotions of the basic-assumption group that he carries all the prestige one would like to believe was the especial perquisite of the work-group leader, it becomes possible to explain some of the disasters into which groups have been led by leaders whose qualifications for the post seem, when the emotions prevalent at their prime have died down, to be devoid of substance.

Freud (1921, p. 45) says that panic is best studied in military groups. I have experienced panic with troops in action on two occasions, and have on several other occasions in small civilian groups had reason to think that the emotional experience bore a sufficiently close resemblance to my military experience to deserve the name panic. I think Freud is discussing the same phenomenon, though these experiences do not appear in all respects to bear out Freud's theories. McDougall's description of panic refers to an experience which I think is similar, in essentials, to my own and I am confirmed in this when he says, 'Other of the cruder, primary emotions may spread through a crowd in very similar fashion though the process is rarely so rapid and intense as in the case of fear' (McDougall, 1920, p. 24), and then describes in a footnote an instance he witnessed in Borneo of the almost instantaneous spread of anger through a crowd (ibid, p. 26). McDougall has thus brought very close together, though without making the connection, anger and fear, and thus supports my view that panic is an aspect of the fight-flight group. It is my contention that panic, flight, and uncontrolled attack are really the same. I am not acquainted with Nestroy's parody, quoted by Freud (1921, p. 49), but taking the story as he gives it, I would agree that it could be taken as typifying panic, but I would say this: there can be no more absolute a way of leaving a battle than by dying. There is nothing in the story of panic flight following the death of the general, that we may regard as incompatible with fidelity to the fight-flight leader; he is followed even when dead, for his death is an act of leadership.

Panic does not arise in any situation unless it is one that might as easily have given rise to rage. The rage or fear are offered no readily available outlet: frustration, which is thus inescapable, cannot be tolerated because frustration requires awareness of the passage of time, and time is not a dimension of basic-assumption phenomena. Flight offers an immediately available opportunity for expression of the emotion in the fight-flight group and therefore meets the demand for instantaneous satisfaction—therefore the group will fly. Alternatively, attack offers a similarly immediate outlet—then the group will fight. The fight-flight group will follow any leader (and, contrary to views hitherto expressed, retains its coherence in doing so) who will give such orders as license instantaneous flight or instantaneous attack. Provided that an individual in the group conforms to the limitations of the fight-flight leader, he will have no difficulty in turning a group from headlong flight to attack or from headlong attack to panic.

The stimulus for panic, or the rage that I consider to be interchangeable, must always be an event that falls outside the work-group functions of the group involved. That is to say, the degree of organization of the group is not a factor in panic unless the organization (which is, as I have said, a part of work-group function) has been evolved for coping with the specific external event responsible for the panic. In Freud's (1921, p. 47) example of a fire in a theatre or place of amusement, the work group is devoted to the watching of play but not to the witnessing of a conflagration, still less to the extinguishing of it. The essential point about organization is that it should be suitable both to the external aim of the group and to the manipulation of the basic assumption that such a pursuit is most calculated to evoke. Panic in an army is not produced by a military danger, though military danger is, in the nature of things, very likely to be present. It is not likely to be produced by any situation in which attack or flight are appropriate expressions of work group. If it appears to arise in such a situation it is because the actual cause is not observed.

It is clear that between the theories advanced by Freud

and those I have sketched out here there is a gap. It may appear to be more considerable than it is because of my deliberate use of a new terminology with which to clothe the apparatus of mechanisms that I think I have detected. It will be necessary to test this by looking at the group more from the standpoint of the individual. But, before I do this, I shall sum up by saying that Freud sees the group as a repetition of part-object relationships. It follows from this that groups would, in Freud's view, approximate to neurotic patterns of behaviour, whereas in my view they would approximate to the patterns of psychotic behaviour.

The society or group that is healthy shows its resemblance to the family group as Freud describes it. The more disturbed the group, the less it is likely to be understood on the basis of family patterns or neurotic behaviour as we know it in the individual.

This does not mean that I consider my descriptions apply only to sick groups. On the contrary, I very much doubt if any real therapy could result unless these psychotic patterns were laid bare with no matter what group. In some groups their existence is early discernible; in others, work has to be done before they become manifest. These groups resemble the analytic patient who appears much more ill after many months of analysis than he did before he had had any analysis at all.

The individual who attends a group for treatment is entitled to believe that he is going to experience something that will lead to his cure. Almost without exception—and the exceptions have themselves to be demonstrated as more apparent than real—patients are convinced that the group is no good and cannot cure them. It is something of a shock to them to find, at any rate when I am a member of the group, that what takes place is not something that allays these anxieties, but appears rather to be a detailed and painstaking demonstration that their vague and ill-formulated suspicions and resentments about the group are based, as often as not, on only too substantial group attitudes towards them and their troubles. Their suspicions are well grounded; they are anchored, at one end at any rate, in what seems to be a perfectly genuine indifference to them, or worse still, hatred of them. For example: A woman is talking in a group consisting, on this occasion, of six people and myself. She complains of a difficulty about food, her fear of choking if she eats at a restaurant, and of her embarrassment at the presence, during a recent meal, of an attractive woman at her table 'I don't feel like that,' says Mr. A, and his remark is met by a murmur of sound from one or two others which could indicate that they were at one with him; could indicate it and does indicate it, but at the same time leaves them free to say, for this group had now become wily, if need arose, that they 'hadn't said anything'. The remainder looked as if the matter were of no interest or concern to them. If a patient spoke in analysis as the woman had spoken, it is clear that according to the state of her analysis the analyst would not expect to have any great difficulty in seeing that a number of interpretations were possible. I cannot see how any of these interpretations, which are based on years of psycho-analytic study of the pair, can possibly be regarded as appropriate to the group; either that, or we have to revise our ideas of what constitutes the analytic situation. In fact the interpretations I gave were concerned almost entirely with pointing out that the material that followed the woman's confidence to the group indicated the group's anxiety to repudiate that the woman's difficulty, whatever it was, was theirs, and furthermore that they were, in that respect, superior to the woman. I was then able to show that the reception the group had given to the woman's candour had now made it very difficult for any of the remainder of the group to speak, individually, of those other respects in which, in a burst of frankness, they were prepared to admit that they were 'inferior'. In short, it was not difficult to show that if a patient did go so far as to come to the group for help with a difficulty, what she got was an increase of feelings of inferiority, and a reinforcement of feelings of loneliness and lack of worth.

Now, this situation is not similar to that which obtains in an analysis when the analyst has succeeded in making overt unconscious fears and anxieties. In the instance that I have given, no interpretation was made that would elucidate for the woman the significance of her anxieties when eating in the presence of 'an attractive woman'. The series of interpretations that I gave could, in so far as they were successful, have made clear to her the disagreeable emotions associated with being the receptor in a group which is resorting freely to projective identification. I could have made clear to her that her 'meal' in the session was causing her embarrassment, and to some extent this was implicit in the interpretations I was giving to the group as a whole. But it seems fair to say that, from an analytic point of view, the woman is not getting a satisfactory interpretation, and is suffering an experience the discomfort of which is not intrinsic to her disability, but inheres in the fact that group treatment is the wrong treatment. There is, however, another possibility, and it is this: when this woman was speaking, although I had no reason to suppose and still do not suppose that she was anything but a case of psycho-neurosis, the whole manner in which she expressed herself reminded me strongly of the candour and coherence of unconscious expression that so often contrasts, in the psychotic, with the confusion that attends his attempts at rational communication. I can make my point clearer by saying that I believe that if this patient had spoken when in analysis with me as she did in the group, her intonation and manner would never have led me to doubt that the correct

interpretation would be one appropriate to a neurotic disability; in the group I felt that manner and intonation alike
indicated that her behaviour would be more accurately
assessed if it were regarded as akin to the formulations of the
psychotic. Regarded in this light I would say that she felt
that there was a single object, called the group, that had been
split up into pieces (the individual members of the group)
by her eating, and that the belief that this was so reinforced
guilty feelings that the emotions associated with being the
receptor of projective identifications were the fault of her
behaviour. These feelings of guilt again made it difficult for
her to understand the part played in her emotions by the
actions of the other members of the group.

So far I have considered the 'badness of the group' as it
touches the patient trying to get treatment; we may now
turn to consider this from the point of view of the members
of the group who have been trying to achieve 'cure' by the
splitting and projective mechanisms described by Melanie
Klein (1946). Not only have they divested themselves of any
of the troubles of the woman patient, but, if this mechanism
is to be effective, they have laid themselves open to the
necessity for getting rid of any sense of responsibility towards the woman. This they do by splitting off good parts of
their personality and placing them in the analyst. In this way
the 'treatment' that these individuals receive from the group
is the achievement of a state of mind recognizably akin to
the 'loss of individual distinctiveness', spoken of by Freud, on
the one hand, and the depersonalization that we meet with
in psychotics, on the other. At this point the group is in the
state I have described as having the basic assumption of
dependence dominant.

I shall not go further with the description of subsequent
development in this group, except to mention one peculiarity
of its subsequent behaviour very common to all kinds of

group situations; subsequent communications were in terms of short interjections, long silences, sighs of boredom, movements of discomfort. This state of affairs in a group deserves close attention. The group appears to be capable of enduring almost endless periods of such conversation, or none at all. There are protests, but endurance of this monotony appears to be a lesser evil than action to end it. It is impossible to give all my reasons for thinking this phase of group behaviour to be significant. I shall content myself with saying that it is closely linked with the splitting and depersonalization mentioned above. I also believe it to be linked with feelings of depression probably in much the same way as maintenance of the schizoid position serves to suppress the depressive position (Klein, 1946).

VERBAL COMMUNICATION

In this state, when interpretations are made, they are disregarded. This disregard may be, as in psycho-analysis, more apparent than real; it may be that the interpretations are faulty and on that account inefficacious; or it may be that the basic assumptions are so dominant that any lead is ignored that does not fall within the limitations of those states. But even allowing for these possibilities, there is an unexplained residue. I have been forced to the conclusion that verbal exchange is a function of the work group. The more the group corresponds with the basic-assumption group the less it makes any rational use of verbal communication. Words serve as a vehicle for the communication of sound. Melanie Klein (1930) has stressed the importance of symbol formation in the development of the individual, and her discussion of the breakdown of a capacity for symbol formation appears to me to be relevant to the group state I am describing. The work group understands that particular use of symbols which is involved in communication; the basic-assumption group does not. I have heard it suggested that the 'language' of the basic-assumption group is primitive. I do not believe this to be true. It seems to me to be debased rather than primitive. Instead of developing lauguage as a method of thought, the group uses an existing language as a mode of action. This 'simplified' method of communication has none of the vitality of primitive or early language. Its simplicity is degenerate and debased. Contrast to this state of affairs is provided by the occasions when a group, aware of the inadequacies of its vocabulary, tries to discuss and agree upon terms which they want to use in the group. In this instance, one might say one sees the evolution of a 'primitive' scientific method as a part of work-group function, but there is nothing debased about it. The 'language' of the basic-assumption group lacks the precision and scope that is conferred by a capacity for the formation and use of symbols: this aid to development is therefore missing, and stimuli that would ordinarily promote development have no effect. But one might well claim for the methods of communication that the group employs the title of Universal Linguistic, which Croce conferred on aesthetics. Every human group instantaneously understands every other human group, no matter how diverse its culture, language, and tradition, on the level of the basic assumptions.

As an exercise in the application of some of the theories I have been putting forward, I will instance the biblical account of the building of the Tower of Babel.[1] The myth brings together—rather in the way that a psycho-analytic patient's associations bring together—the following com-

---

[1] Genesis xi. 1-9. This account is a part of the so-called Jahvistic code and could therefore be regarded as an example of recording by a group with dependent basic assumption dominant when threatened by the emergence of the basic assumption of pairing.

ponents: a universal language; the building by the group of a tower which is felt by the Deity to be a menace to his position; a confounding of the universal language and a scattering abroad of the people on the face of the earth. What kind of event is embedded in this myth? I shall use my theories to interpret the myth as embodying an account of the development of language in a group with the dependent basic assumption dominant. The new development—it is worth remembering that Freud chose the development of language as an instance of group activity of high mental order—in itself demands further development in the group; this I take to be implicit in the symbolism of the tower, the building of which menaces the supremacy of the Deity. The idea that the tower would reach to Heaven introduces the element of Messianic hope which I regard as intrinsic to the pairing group. But a Messianic hope that is fulfilled violates the canon of the pairing basic assumption, and the group dissolves in schisms.

Melanie Klein (1930) has shown that the inability to form symbols is characteristic of certain individuals, I would extend this to include all individuals in their functions as members of the basic-assumption group.

SUMMARY

Freud's view of the dynamics of the group seem to me to require supplementation rather than correction. There are many occasions when the apposite interpretation is one that draws attention to behaviour in the group that would be appropriate if it were a reaction to a family situation. In other words there is ample evidence for Freud's idea that the family group provides the basic pattern for all groups. If I have not stressed the evidence for this, it is because that view does not seem to me to go far enough. I doubt whether any attempt to establish a group therapeutic procedure can be successful if it is limited to an investigation of mechanisms deriving from this source. I would go further; I think that the central position in group dynamics is occupied by the more primitive mechanisms that Melanie Klein has described as peculiar to the paranoid-schizoid and depressive positions. In other words I feel, but would not like to be challenged with my limited experience to prove, that it is not simply a matter of the incompleteness of the illumination provided by Freud's discovery of the family group as the prototype of all groups, but the fact that this incompleteness leaves out the source of the main emotional drives in the group.

It may be, of course, that this is an artefact produced by the frustration of the individual's desire to be alone with me in the group. I do not wish to minimize the importance of this, but in fact I do not believe that the phenomena I have witnessed are peculiar to a therapeutic group. All groups stimulate and at the same time frustrate the individuals composing them; for the individual is impelled to seek the satisfaction of his needs in his group and is at the same time inhibited in this aim by the primitive fears that the group arouses.

To recapitulate: any group of individuals met together for work shows work-group activity, that is, mental functioning designed to further the task in hand. Investigation shows that these aims are sometimes hindered, occasionally furthered, by emotional drives of obscure origin. A certain cohesion is given to these anomalous mental activities if it is assumed that emotionally the group acts as if it had certain basic assumptions about its aims. These basic assumptions, which appear to be fairly adequately adumbrated by three formulations, dependence, pairing, and fighting or flight, are, on further investigation, seen to displace each other, as if in response to some unexplained impulse. They appear, furthermore, to have some common link, or, perhaps, even to be different aspects of each other. Further investigation shows that each basic assumption contains features that correspond so closely with extremely primitive part objects that sooner or later psychotic anxiety, appertaining to these primitive relationships, is released. These anxieties, and the mechanisms peculiar to them, have been already displayed in psycho-analysis by Melanie Klein, and her descriptions tally well with the emotional states that find an outlet in mass action of the group in behaviour that seems to have coherence if it is considered to be the outcome of a basic assumption. Approached from the angle of sophisticated work-group activity, the basic assumptions appear to be the source of emotional drives to aims far different either from the overt task of the group or even from the tasks that would appear to be appropriate to Freud's view of the group as based on the family group. But approached from the angle of psychotic anxiety associated with phantasies of primitive part-object relationships, described by Melanie Klein and her co-workers, the basic-assumption phenomena appear far more to have the characteristics of defensive reactions to psychotic anxiety, and to be not so much at variance with Freud's views as supplementary to them. In my view, it is necessary to work through both the stresses that appertain to family patterns and the still more primitive anxieties of part-object relationships. In fact I consider the latter to contain the ultimate sources of all group behaviour.

If it is felt that the attempt to establish a group therapeutic procedure as a method for treating the individual is worth while, psycho-analysts would be well advised to find a new name for it. I cannot see that there is any scientific justification for describing work of the kind I have attempted as psycho-analysis—I have already given my reasons for this (pp. 178-82). In addition to this there is the fact, of which we are all aware, that bitter experience has taught us that resistance against the unconscious can be so subtle that it may distort the analytical findings and reinterpret them in support of some personal defence (Jones, 1952) and therefore the term psycho-analysis should continue to be applied, in so far as we can control the situation, to the fundamental principles of psycho-analysis. There remains the question of what therapeutic value is to be attached to the procedure I have tried to describe. I do not think that the time has come to give a definite opinion, and I believe that there may be room for fully qualified psycho-analysts to carry on research into its value, possibly with groups composed of individuals who themselves are having or have had a psycho-analysis.

As a description of group dynamics, each individual is in a position to decide for himself whether the theories I have adumbrated give meaning to the phenomena which he, in the course of his daily life as a member of a group, can witness.

REFERENCES

FORTES MEYER (1949). 'Time and Social Structure: an Ashanti Case Study.' In *Social Structure*. Oxford: Clarendon Press.

FREUD, S. (1911). 'Formulations on the two Principles of Mental Functioning.' London: Hogarth Press. *Collected Papers*, Vol. IV; *The Complete Psychological Works of Sigmund Freud*, Vol 12.

FREUD, S. (1913). *Totem and Taboo*. London: Hogarth Press, 1950. *Complete Works*, Vol. 13.

FREUD, S. (1921). *Group Psychology and the Analysis of the Ego*. 1922. London: Hogarth Press. *Complete Works*, Vol. 18.

FREUD, S. (1930). *Civilization and its Discontents*. London and New York, 1930. *Complete Works*, Vol. 21.

HEIMANN, PAULA (1952a). 'Certain Functions of Introjection and Projection in Early Infancy.' In Klein *et al.* (eds.) *Developments in Psycho-Analysis.* London: Hogarth Press, 1952.

HEIMANN, PAULA (1952b). 'A Contribution to the Re-evaluation of the Oedipus Complex—the Early Stages.' *Int. J. Psycho-Anal. Vol. 23, Pt. 2. Also in Klein et al.* (eds.) *New Directions in Psycho-Analysis*; London: Tavistock Publications, 1955; New York: Basic Books.

JONES, ERNEST (1952). Preface to *Developments in Psycho-Analysis.* London: Hogarth Press.

KLEIN, MELANIE (1928). 'Early Stages of the Oedipus Complex.' In *Contributions to Psycho-Analysis, 1921-1945.* London: Hogarth Press, 1948.

KLEIN, MELANIE (1930). 'The Importance of Symbol-Formation in the Development of the Ego.' In *Contributions to Psycho-Analysis.* London: Hogarth Press, 1948.

KLEIN, MELANIE (1935). 'A Contribution to the Psychogenesis of Manic-Depressive States.' In *Contributions to Psycho-Analysis.* London: Hogarth Press, 1948.

KLEIN MELANIE (1945). 'The Oedipus Complex in the Light of Early Anxieties.' In *Contributions to Psycho-Analysis.* London: Hogarth Press, 1948.

KLEIN, MELANIE (1946). 'Notes on Some Schizoid Mechanisms.' In Klein *et al.* (eds.), *Developments in Psycho-Analysis.* London: Hogarth Press, 1952.

McDOUGALL, W. (1920). *The Group Mind.* (2nd ed.) London: Cambridge University Press, 1927.

TROTTER, W. (1916). *Instincts of the Herd in Peace and War.* London.

LE BON, G. (1896). *The Crowd: a Study of the Popular Mind* London: Benn, 1947.

Index

co-operation, 90, 116, 136
counter-transference, 149-50
Croce, 186

dancing class,
  formation of a, 20
dependent group *see also baD*, 74,
    78-86, 119-22, 166
  basic assumptions, 147
  group deity in, 148, 166
  pathological leadership in, 121-2
  pull away from, 91
  religion and, 85-6
  St. Augustine and, 129-30
  security in, 94
  specialized work group and, 156,
    157, 158
  tuberculosis and, 107
  Welfare State and 126
  work group and, 99-100
depersonalization, 184, 185
depressive position, 8, 164, 185,
    188
development,
  basic assumptions, time and, 158-
    60
discipline for the neurotic, 12-15
disease *see also group diseases*,
  study of, 110
'dual',
  of dependent group, 119-22
  of situations, 87-90

Early stages of the Oedipus Con-
    flict, 164
Einzig,
  on currency, 110
emotional oscillation in a group,
    124-6

family, the,
  group and, 69, 181, 187-8, 189
father, 69
fearfulness, 81
fight-flight group, 63, 64, 65, 67, 71,
    72, 73, 74, 75, 97, 152, 160
  dependent group and, 81, 82, 91
  leadership of, 161, 177, 180
  security in, 94-5

fight-flight group (cont.)
  specialized work group and, 156,
    157, 158
flight *see fight-flight group*
food difficulties,
  a woman patient's, 182-4
Fortes, Meyer,
  on social structure, 172
Freud, 127, 141, 143, 153n, 156n,
    174, 175
cit., 184
  critique of discussion of groups
    by, 134
  on family and the group, 165,
    187, 188, 189
  on individual and group psy-
    chology, 130-1, 167-8
  on individual and the group, cit.,
    135, 170
  on language and the group, 187
  on leader of the group, 177
  on libidinous nature of the
    group, 176
  on McDougall and the group,
    cit., 135, 171
  on panic and the group, 179, 180
  on part-object relationships and
    the group, 181
  on regression and the group, cit.,
    142
  on social instinct, 131
  transference and, 104, 136
frustration in groups, 54

Genesis XI. 1-9, 186n
gestures,
  communication by, 70
Gibbon, 100
God, 122, 124, 130, 147, 148
'good group spirit', 25-6
'goodness', 93
greed,
  guilt in 'dependent' group about,
    74
group analysis *see group therapy*
    (analysis)
and psychiatrist (group) (analyst)
group culture, 55, 56, 57, 59-60, 61,
    66, 71, 73
  changes, 73

group deity,
  dependent group and, 148, 166
  psychiatrist as, 99-100
group diseases, 102-3, 105-6
group dynamics, 141-91
group mentality, 50, 52-3, 54, 55,
    56-7, 59, 60, 61
  definition of, 65
group psychology,
  essential nature of, 131-2
  individual psychology and, 130-1,
    134, 167-8
*Group Psychology and the Analysis
    of the Ego*, 130, 141n
group, the
  essential prerequisites of, 132-3,
    168
group therapy (analysis) *see also
psychiatrist (group) (analyst)*
  application of in a small ward,
    23-6
  army organization of, 16-17
  definition of, 11
  discussions (examples), 41-3, 46-7,
    51-2
  genesis of, 29
  psycho-analysis and, 80-1, 93,
    115, 121
  psycho-analysis and final assess-
    ment of, 189-90
  psycho-analysis and (a woman's
    food difficulties), 182-4
  tensions in, 11-26
  therapeutic group concept, 75
  therapeutic value of, 190

Halliday, 108
hallucinations,
  group situation and production
    of, 56
hate, 68, 70, 75
hatred of learning by experience,
    86-91
Heimann, Paula, 164, 164n
herd, the,
  identification with, 89, 90
  instinct, 168, 169
Hobbes, 130
homoousian controversy, 100

hope, 151-2
hostility in the group, 69, 70, 84
Human Relations, 7
individual psychology, 131
  group psychology and, 134, 167-8

individual, the
  basic and sophisticated group
    and, 96
  dilemma of, and the group,
    117-19
  fearfulness and, in dependent
    group, 81
  Freud on, group and, cit., 135
  group and, 52, 53, 54, 56, 57, 59,
    61, 64, 65, 74, 129, 188
  'groupishness' of, 131, 132, 133,
    168, 169
  independence and submergence
    of in the group, 90-1
  McDougall, cit., on, 175
  proto-mental phenomena and, 103
  security in the group and, 96
  valency and, 116-7
individual treatment,
  group and, 80
intellectual activity (ability,
    capacity), 175
interpretations *see under psy-
    chiatrist (group) (analyst)*
introjection,
  group and, 164
  leader and, 177

jealousy, 75
Jones, Ernest,
  on unconscious, cit., 190

Kephron, (Pharaoh), 120, 121
King Saul, 124
Klein, Melanie, 8, 141, 149, 162n,
    164, 164n, 169n, 177, 184, 185,
    187, 188, 189

language, 186
  Tower of Babel and develop-
    ment of group, 187
Le Bon, 131, 141, 167
  Freud's critique of, 134-5, 169-70